A PILLAR OF A VICTORY BEATING DRUM

Maryalice Swiney-Zoe

Jungle Boogie Ink

A PILLAR OF A VICTORY BEATING DRUM

Excerpts from the King James Version of the bible, published by the
World Publishing Company in Cleveland and New York. Excerpts are
from II Timothy 4:7, John 16:13-15, Ephesians 1:3, 11,13,18,19, Isaiah
32:2, Acts 3:16, Psalm 23, Psalm 127:3-5, Romans 5:3-5, and Daniel 3:28.
All rights reserved.
ISBN: 099793610X
ISBN: 978-0-9979361-1-7 EBook Version
ISBN: 9780997936100 Paperback Version

Printed in the United States of America
Jungle Boogie Ink Paperbacks/ July 2016
Second Edition
Jungle Boogie Ink Paperbacks are published by Jungle Boogie Ink, 3894
Crenshaw Blvd. Unit 561495, Los Angeles, CA 90056.

PRAISE FOR PILLAR OF A VICTORY BEATING DRUM

"Very intriguing and captivating story. It draws you in where you become a part of the quest for survival. The main character, Caesar's life was the beatin' drum which ended in victory. His grandfather embedded in him the history of their family's strength and survival through slavery. He instilled in him the three important rhythms to the beatin' drum: support, approach and influence."

—Janice Woods, Inspired Writer and Real Estate Broker, Real Estate Solutions by Jan Marie

"Maryalice book is a very passionate outline of the history of the Swiney Family dating back to 1865. A page turning story. I really enjoyed reading this book from start to finish. Each chapter is very well written, the chapters were so detailed and vivid that it gave me the sense that I was there witnessing what was happening first hand. The poems were very powerful."

— Lynn V. Hanks

"I love reading the true story…The story took be back to when I was growing up in the South and the challenges of trials and tribulations I had to face in the 1940's. The story is an Internal beginning of strength and an ending of true faith."

—*Della Jackson and Friends Book Club, L.A.*

"I had the opportunity to review many of Swiney-Zoë short stories books and I highly recommend them. Readers will love reading A Pillar of a Victory Beating Drum. The story is a learning based on strength, trials, and tribulations. I couldn't put Swiney-Zoë's book down. It is the most riveting; powerful book I have ever read. Very well written, challenging, captivating, and inspiring at the same time, the story will also move you too. I'm was so glad the character Caesar had the courage to beat the odds to live and to believe God and faith. The story gave me a whole new understanding of the impossible can be powerful by faith."

—*The Mystery, Drama and Poetry Review*

"Historical, passionate, powerful."

—*Book Listing*

"Couldn't put it down. The story kept me informed that faith is possible if one believes in the truthiness of strength. The story, poems, and songs kept me wanting to read more."

—Star and Strength Book Club *(4 ½ stars)*

"Wonderfully written, heartfelt story of survival and resilience. It will captivate until you don't want to put this put this book down. The story is a guide to search for strength, hope, and willingness. An empowering, compelling novel with a strong message. The story is an invaluable resource for anyone seeking faith in any challenges he or she has been faced with in life. It is a book that offers answers to hope."

—*Andrew's Independent Research of African American and Diaspora History Review*

"The story, poems, and songs are powerful and lasting...Our book club members loved the story from prologue to the last page and the book was hard to put down. The book club really loved this book. It is a powerful true story of overcoming incredible odds. Swiney-Zoë's writing is amazing."

—*K and S Readers Drama Book Club*

"A candid look at the life of a young boy—inspiring and an historic journey. Reading the story of Caesar's journey, copy of the journal, and hospital notes inspired me to write a journal."

—Terry

"POWERFUL AND INTRIGUING."

—*L.A. Chapter Review*

"The story is a whole new understanding that the impossible can be powerful by faith."

—*The Mystery, Drama and Poetry Review*

"Swiney-Zoë changes the style in writing. The story is only one of its kind and intriguing of a black man to be survive and tragic accident in the 1920s. The story of Caesar is heroic inspiring."

—*Faith and Healing Review*

"I enjoyed this read because it simply followed the family's life with powerful inspiration intertwined with the story. It was very realistic in the sense that there was no traditional plot, but small series that were interconnected."

—Lulu, *Goodreads.com*

"The author tells a rich vivid history of the trials and tribulations of Caesar, a black man growing up and over coming racism and serious health issues in the midst of the 30s and 40s who led by faith filled life with conviction that has carried him to build the family he has today..."

—Kari Chambers

"A Pillar of a Victory Beating Drum is a wonderful and passionate story about family, strength, faith, purpose and determination. The story that draws you in and is easy for anyone with their own family to understand."

—Corinthian Jackson

ACKNOWLEDGMENTS

Thank you to the high and mighty, our God, Lord, and Savior Jesus Christ for his work of prosperity. Second, my editor Lisa-Marie, thank you for your hard work, advice, professionalism, and encouragement, while I developed this manuscript.

But I would be thoughtless if I did not give special thanks to my great-grandfather Charles Swiney II and grandfather Dingus Swiney for writing such a detailed journal that told the story of the Great Depression. Thank you, to my father Cesar Swiney for giving me the inheritance of your life, the journal, and the history of our African ancestors.

Thank you to the doctors at Charity Hospital. Medicine is a window of opportunity; for that, I am grateful for your service. Charity Hospital's Dr. Kay Kohara, thank you for your service and commitment to saving lives.

'Adieu', to my piano teacher Ms. Consuelo Pappy. Finally, thank you to my mother for encouraging me to complete the book; storms came and storms went.

ASHIKO: ENGLISH VERSION

Hear us our Father,
Come roll your sea.

Our Lord's salvation,
Well, we hear our Lord,
Coming goes into the sea.

On dry land,
My Lord our Ashiko beating drums!
Come roll your sea.

Your children drown,
In the misty water like a stone,
King of Kings. Lord of Lords,
Come roll your sea.

Breathe your air,
Heaven, goes the wind,
Will, our Lord, Ashiko beating drums!
Roll the water on the earth.

PROLOGUE

P atience, reality and the faith to live is innate to humanity. Crashing waves, a puddle of broken water covers the old wooden floor, while a gray rope of twisted thread remains attached from the infant to its mother's womb. Internally, our triumph as builders is inheriting our ancestor's history that connects us to our trials and challenges. The obstacle of pain for the will to our victories is the reality of our journeys in life. Continuous rhythm for strength always beats loudly and rejoices fully.

Now authentically, our memoirs and our journeys of rhythmic victories will always build rapidly our faith every day for every second and every minute. Heed closely, as I speak for a moment to my authentic journey:

My mother's strength of wisdom;
She is our giver of life;

Yet, the heavens face is clearly patient.
And I continue to be patient,
I will soon inherit many challenges.

To God's rhythmic power of good?
The master that I serve is authentic.
The solid rock; He is the waves of broken trust,
The muffle sounds of the Ashiko.

The time has come to enter the world,
To learn, to find a path of strength,
Importantly, to listen to the Ashiko tone,
The three tones.
The beating drums.

Restlessly in my mother's womb,
Time is running short,
To great my family.

A dark color girl with long wavy hair,
A dark color boy with wiry hair,
A boy that is bright as light,
Importantly, a loud wooly girl with pigtails;
She in particular, I have been warned by counsel,
My triumphs must not be her victories.

My curiosity of a slender, tall, dark color man,
With black wiry hair, black mustache,

And medium brown skin.
Light blue shirt, and heavy working shoes,
With the smell of tobacco, that scents his body;
He is ordained with strength and courage.

The smell of lumber covers his body each day.
I must benefit from his work.
On the seventh day, he wears a black jacket,
White shirt, black pants, and black shoes.

His mind never restricted and oppressed,
My encouragement to him;
He walks with the Ashiko beating drum.

A woman that carries my body,
With dark eyes, long hair that falls to her hips.
Her shoulders always stride back;
Her high cheekbones, a pair of warm dark eyes,
The scent of perfume that florist her skin.

For nine months,
She knows my character best.

The family table always bare,
Wooden plates, bowls, and spoons,
Lay flat on a wood nook shelf.
Fortunately, the fragile lumber,
Always holds the house together.

A body of clay is from my creator's work,
Yet, his hands carry my struggles;
His drum beats hard with all rights.
His word is my armor to victory,
My hunger and thirst is his victory.

Our ancestors their deepest battles,
And their struggles,
The journeys they endured,
Are inheritance by memories of our elders.

God, the Father of Jesus Christ our Lord,
The seed of David;
For our Father is powerful and victorious.
Time is running out to summon our Father.
Internally, the counsel has forewarned me.

The journey of our faith is the challenge that has been passed down by our elders and our ancestors. The victories from our faith are our trials and bravery. When we have failed at our work, we become crippled. When we have become lost within our challenges, we have become lost in God's word.

The anointed wickedness from our own blood is wounding, for the thirst and hunger to victory does not beat without internal strength and faith. When we are given treasury of our ancestors, we at that point can write our journey of our triumphs.

Our failures, our patience, our loss of antiquity, and our journeys have quilts of triumphs…Our victories are to become a better servant to God with no limits. In all of our failures and all of our victories, there is always the authentic and internal light.

Hence, our failures in life become our hunger to acknowledge God, our Lord, and Savior Jesus Christ; our thirst is our commitment to faith.

God gives us internal strength, internal and authentic encouragements with words of belief and trust.

No person's external drum beats as loud as God's victory drum. The word of the challenging journeys, true listening is always a passion of commitment and determination to live and learn.

CHAPTER 1

JOURNEY OF A THOUSAND MILES

"Henry! Henreeeeee!" It was the voice of a twelve-year-old blind girl name Ellen, calling her brother across the dusty road. A tall, slender, attractive woman with jet-black hair was lifting a bundle of clothes to a bench, and placing them in the three supporting tubs. It was Monday, washday.

With a basket of clothes, Rosie walked to the wash-house located across the street from her sister-in-law Lucy's house.

Easing her slender body gently into an open space between the tubs filled with water, Rosie placed a small bundle of clothes in a barrel of hot water. She sprinkled powder soap in the barrel of hot water. She placed a

wet shirt on a washboard and began scrubbing the shirt using a manual turnkey with a wooden handle. Rosie repeatedly does this to all the clothes.

After scrubbing, making sure the clothes were clean, she puts each piece of clothing in a barrel of boiling hot water for sterilization.

Rosie turns, shading her eyes with her hand, making the syllable snap, "HENRY!" she yelled.

"I'm a comin'." This was Henry's standard response to any call.

Grabbing his nearest companion's cap, Henry tossed it into the sky, laughing. He headed in the direction of sister's call, hurried on his way by a hail of rocks thrown by his friends, a game that could wait.

"Boy, don't you hear yore sista callin' you? Lord, these children, gets to playin' and can't hear a thing." These words Rosie intended for Ms. Mary to hear. Ms. Mary struggled with a bundle of laundry much larger than Rosie's bundle of clothes.

"Mornin' Rosie. Here it's near nine o'clock, and I haven't gotten started on this wash yet," Ms. Mary said, sweeping Rosie an absent-minded glance that came to rest on the wooden house that sat across the street from the wash shed.

"Mornin' Ms. Mary," Rosie responded.

"This hot weatha is gonna be hard on her," Ms. Mary gestured, nodding her head to the house that Dingus and Lucy Sweeney occupied. Ms. Mary counted the number of Sweeney children, "is this her fourth or fifth child?"

How hard it was for Ms. Mary to keep count of all the children in the neighborhood was a matter of her opinion. About the weather, there could be none, for it was hot as it could be in July, the kind of heat that sapped the body and parched the skin. It seemed to bake a person from within. To sweat in this sort of heat was one of life's little pleasures. A cool breeze at the end of the day was one of heaven's greatest gifts that rarely happened unless there was a thunderstorm brewing. Especially, the quick ones that seemed to appear out of a sparkling blue sky garnished with dark fluffy clouds. These storms never caught anyone by surprise, for storms can be felt.

"HENRY!" Ellen calling her brother again.

"Mommy wants you, she says hurry," Ellen said.

"I's here," Henry responded.

From the strained look on his mother's' face, with her strong mulatto features, Henry sensed this was important. What Henry loved best was to run errands for his mother.

He would earn pennies for these errands. He would take great pleasure in this whenever he got the chance.

"Momma, cans I—"

"Not now Henry, run and tell yore daddy to come home, and don't tarry long," Lucy said, grasping her stomach in severe pain as the sweat rolled down her tan face.

Dashing across an open field, leading through the woods was a scribble walk pathway, Henry lingered along his way to the Company. There were a few bright spots of sunlight for him to enjoy.

Nearing the Company, Henry saw his Uncle Rush returning a friendly wave and a cheerful smile.

The Company or the hard mill was the sole reason for the extension of the small-town of Shreveport.

The lumber was transported to the mill to be sawed into various sizes, and then sold to lumbering companies throughout the country.

The sweet scent from the fresh-cut lumber was a sign that God's creation was at work. Henry felt that he could pick up more tips on how the sawmill worked, for he knew that someday he would operate one. His father, Dingus had worked at various sections of the Company since moving from Georgia where he had sharecropped. Retiring from sharecropping, Dingus had moved his wife Lucy and their four kids to Shreveport after hearing that there was work at the mill. After learning the jobs assigned to him and showing an aptitude for learning, Dingus was allowed to operate the cut off saw. That raised his confidence.

He believed that he had done the right thing in leaving the sharecropping business behind and seeking employment at the Company.

The high-pitched hum and whine of the saw had to be used with rhythm and concentration. With the slow movement of his hands, Dingus moved a deck of lumber into position. Not losing his concentration, Dingus glided the lumber across the sharp, fast blade. Dingus rotated the tension handle clockwise until the blade became tighter.

He began sawing another set of lumber. This left a beautiful piece of smooth hardwood ready to build homes or wherever there was a demand for the lumber.

As he continued his assigned tasks, he thought about building houses, cabinets, and furniture. These would be some of the thoughts running through his head, maybe even building a better home for his wife Lucy and the children. These were some many dreams Dingus had for the future.

He was abruptly brought back to reality when he noticed his son Henry standing beside him, fascinated with his working of the saw. Henry had forgotten what he had come to tell his father.

"Hi, daddy. Momma says fo you to come home, she doesn't feels well," Henry said. Without asking any questions, Dingus knew what he had to do. Placing his rough hand on his son's head, he gave it a playful shake.

"Okay son, runs long home. I'll be home shortly. I have to tell the boss," Dingus said.

"Now we can get on with the game," Henry thought. Shutting down the sawmill, Dingus headed for the supervisor's office to ask permission to be absent for the rest of the day.

Mr. Clayton, a kindly white man, would surely understand. The men under his supervision took the liberty of shortening his name to Clay, with his permission of course.

"Lucy's time has come. I have to fetch Aunt Phoebe," Dingus thought.

Looking up from the papers on his desk, Clay saw Dingus approaching the office. Clay had a smirk on his face, swatting a fly that landed on the windowsill.

"Lucy's time has come. I need to goes home and be with her," Dingus said nervously.

"All right I suppose. How many does this make? You have betta be careful, or you won't have a place at the dinner table. Be here early tomorrow. We don't want to get behind with this order," Clay said, half-smile on his face, and then returned back to read the newspaper.

"Tell Ivory to take your place and send Morris to the office," Clay said.

Dingus removed his gloves and said what was expected of him, "Yessir. Thank you, sir." Dingus walked out of the office making eye contact with his twin brother Rush, who was stacking lumber with another Company employee.

Walking around the corner of the huge stacks, Dingus noticed that his son stopped to chat with Uncle Rush.

"Good," Dingus thought to himself. Rush had added instructions for his nephew Henry to return home, nodding to Rush in agreement.

"Rush, I have to goes home to be with Lucy. I have to fetch Aunt Phoebe. I was gonna ask you, but I send it by Henry. I will lose some money, but that can't be helped."

Still lingering around the hard mill, Dingus called Henry back to deliver a message to Emma.

"Go by yore Aunt Emma's house and ask her to go stay with your motha 'til I get home. Leave quickly," Dingus ordered Henry.

"I'll ask Mr. Clay if you cans work with me Saturday," Rush said.

"Where's Ivory?" Dingus asked.

"I think he's ten aisles over there," Rush replied, pointing to aisles of cut stacked lumber.

"Aw hell, this will take me out of the way," gestured Dingus. Getting home to his wife was his priority, but the message that he was ordered to deliver could not be ignored. Dingus accepted there was a heap of other problems in this world that had no solution.

After relaying the message, Dingus headed toward the southeast of town in the general direction of Aunt Phoebe's farm where she lived with her two sons.

Aunt Phoebe had the same boarded, wooden house since the death of her husband some sixteen years ago. Dingus knew her sons well, for he would sometimes employ the oldest son to help him turn the garden's dry grass and dirt. Lucy's garden was the one thing she insisted on attending to since their marriage ten years ago.

CHAPTER 2
A PATH APPEARS

Walking at a moderate pace, Dingus ignored the buzzing insects and the scurrying of lizards disturbing his passing through the deep woods. He continued his walk at a moderate pace in the hot sun while removing a sandwich from a brown paper bag that Lucy had fixed him before leaving for work that morning. Walking and eating his sandwich, Dingus crossed a dusty road leading to Catfish Lake. He thought about the many tasks that he had not gotten around to, including Lucy's garden. Having a large family weighed heavily on his mind, Dingus hoped this birth would bring another boy into the world.

Coming up to Catfish Lake, Dingus noticed three women in their mid-sixties on the far side fishing. It appeared that the three women had been fishing at Catfish Lake for some time that day. At that time, he had realized that he had walked three miles, with two more miles to go. He stopped for a moment to remove his shoes, brushing them off with his bare hands. He examined the wear and tear of the shoes. He had procrastinated making himself a new pair of shoes.

Continuing his walk home, an occasional breeze brought a soothing relief to the sweat dripping down his face and chest, and the thirst for water in his throat. He was not particularly worried about Lucy. He knew his wife was a strong woman with courage. Her strength and courage came with the African and mulatto features—

Henry unhurriedly continued his travel to his aunt's house. As he walked through the woods, he took advantage of the shade and grass. Seeing some of his playmates swimming in the lake,

"Hey! What y'all doin'?" Henry yelled.

"You know," the playmates answered, making swimming motions.

His friends invited him to swim with them in the lake.

"Aw, I can't right now, busy. See y'all all later," Henry answered back with regret of taking up the duty of delivering a message.

Picking up a handful of pebbles, Henry hurled pebbles at his friends.

His friends retaliated with a hail of rocks that encouraged him to run, where he finally arrived at his Aunt Emma's house.

CHAPTER 3
SUMMONING

Leaping over Aunt Emma's prized possession, a bush of jasmine flowers, there was a swift force of sweet jasmine scents that covered the air. Exalted and out of breath, Henry stumbled on his words to tell the news to Aunt Emma.

"Mama's not feelin' well. She's havin' uh baby!" Henry said historically out of breath.

"Did you summons yore Father, spiritually?" Aunt Emma asked.

"Yes ma'am."

"I had plan goin' swimmin' with my friends," Henry said disappointed.

He pondered for a moment, whether he could perhaps have the moment to go swimming with his friends.

"Henry, there's no time fore that today. Besides some rain is comin' soon. Not today, Henry," Aunt Emma said.

"Yes ma'am. Daddy say—" His father's message came with a distraction from the loud cracking thunder that echoed the partly blue and gray skies.

"Looks like rain comin' Henry," Aunt Emma said, while preparing lunch in the kitchen, and pondering over the surprising cracking thunder.

Aunt Emma handed Henry a sandwich, with a slice of cake, placed on a small wooden plate, and a glass of milk. He looked forward to each time he ran errands for his mother and father when visiting his fifteen-year-old aunt. She was a seasoned baker of cakes and cookies.

What Henry did not know was that the buttering up of a sandwich, lemonade, and slice of cake would entail another trip to the hard mill.

The summer weather that particular day would soon bring muggy weather. Aunt Emma would fill a kettle bucket with fresh pumped cold water from a water well.

"After you eat lunch, take the kettle bucket of cold water to the hard mill fore the men," Aunt Emma said, pointing to a filled kettle of water sitting on the front door steps.

His face became alarmed, but he hid his irritation, for he had suffered previous from one of her sharp head slaps.

Although Henry failed in going swimming with his friend, he would indulge in one of his other pastimes, hanging out at the Company with the men. Drenched in sweat, he returned to the Company with the cold kettle bucket of water.

"Henry, help me carry this lumber," Uncles Rush ordered Henry.

The remainder of the day at the Company consisted of Henry handing the men fresh cups of cold water—

It was the end of the day at the hard mill. Closing around six o'clock that evening, a cloudburst darkened the skies. A quick storm was coming and it was coming fast.

Henry accompanied his Uncle Rush home, both walking east where the Company housed their employees some five miles from the mill. The dark clouds quickly covered the skies. Walking home, the clouds followed the shadows of Uncle Rush and Henry's souls, arranging and adapting to the sound of their footsteps.

The quick pounding of orchestrated movement from Henry's feet sparked a cord with Uncle Rush. Uncle Rush encouraged Henry to excel in life. For the employment at the hard mill would be a bad investment for his future.

Despite the fair extent of a larger regional phenomenon in the Reconstruction in the south, the timber industry was beginning to lose its purpose. Built lumber company towns became dismantled towns.

CHAPTER 4
LIFE IN AN UNCOMMON WAY

Known to everyone in town as 'Big Mary', she was the town's latest news commentator and the baby forecaster for soon to be mothers. Ms. Mary continued washing at the washhouse, she was concerned about Lucy; for Rosie never returned to the washhouse. This was the first time Rosie ever left her unwashed clothes…

"I wonder how Lucy's doin'. I'se betta look in on her. This wash can wait. This is a bad time to have a baby, it's too hot," she mumbled. Fanning herself off with her hands.

Ms. Mary saw Rosie walking with a pail of water into the Sweeney's house, and Ellen sitting on the steps that led into the house.

"Where's yore momma?" Ms. Mary asked. Not waiting for an answer from Ellen, she walked into the house, one of many typical Company houses built around 1900.

She found Lucy sitting on the back porch her husband had built with a screen door. It also served as an extra bedroom that was built from unsalable lumber from the Company. The room was needed for the growing family. Lucy was sitting in her rocking chair with a pan of green beans that she was preparing for supper.

"How you doin'?" Ms. Mary asked Lucy.

Looking up at Ms. Mary, "Not bad, it's jes' this weather. I have to get these green beans ready fore the girls to cook," Lucy replied in a Louisiana accent. Lucy fanned her face with her hands, struggling to cool herself off.

"How is you Mary?" Ms. Mary reached for one of the straw fans.

"I'm fine, but Shorty's stills ailin'," Ms. Mary said referring to her husband of forty years and fanning herself vigorously. This only caused Ms. Mary to perspire more. Changing the subject from her husband to Lucy, "Lord Lucy, you sure can grow a garden," Ms. Mary said. This compliment of Lucy's garden prompted an indulgent, bright smile. Although Lucy was in pain, she did not take Ms. Mary's kind words to heart. Lucy's secret of her beautiful garden was the water tap that the Company installed behind the backyards of every fourth house in the colored section of Louisiana. The Sweeney family was one of the fortunate black people to have a water tap placed in the backyard.

"How much time does you have?" Ms. Mary asked, shifting her weight in the chair that started to squeak and cry in protest.

"Soon, I think," her reply came in a soft voice, and at the same time she managed to smooth over a short pain in her right hip.

"This weather is no good for birthin'."

Not focusing on the conversation, "Oh, I don' know, I manage," Lucy replied, holding the left side of her hip, and sweat rolling down her smoothed brown skin. After a while, talking about nothing, in particular, Ms. Mary hefted herself to her feet. The chair belched out a loud squeaky sound of relief.

"Well, I betta be gettin' back to my washin'." Having got the information, she had come for, "Shorty is gonna be need'n clean work clothes soon. The doctor say he could go back to work soon. All those doctors know how to do is push pills and mix cough syrup," Ms. Mary complained.

As she walked through the house, the hard wood floor groaned.

Lucy did not appreciate Ms. Mary's surprise visit. She always believed that visiting a neighbor should be in the afternoon, when there was time for that sort of thing. Lucy struggled back into the house, grasping her stomach and giving herself strength to move about in the house. "Becky, here girl. Wash these off, but not too much, they need cookin' for just a short time. Should be done before dinna. You can start the corn bread 'bout the same time."

Ellen helped her mother as she struggled to the bedroom. Lucy closed her eyes to ease the agonizing pain in the lower part of her back and right hip. There would be an occasional burst of pain, most being of a dull variety.

With a faint humorous smile from the corner of her mouth, and not being aware, Lucy drifted into a deep sleep. She would need her strength for the coming delivery that would be long. She would have to search, deep down, in her soul to survive.

CHAPTER 5

RAY OF LIGHT

Dingus continued his travel home, walking pass Catfish Lake. He furthered his walk, passing some lumber that lay rested across a now dry-washed lake. A flock of birds, hopping rabbits, and the beam of sunlight crossed his pathway. For a testament of God's work is what the family would need.

Among animals, there was a purpose in a man's journey to design, to discover what God has given, to enjoy and to appreciate for what he included for man.

A sprinkle of a ray of light showered the tall leafy trees while the wind blew a cool breeze. He used this welcome shade for most of the remaining walk to Aunt Phoebe's house. To the left side of the woody trail there stood an old oak tree. Resting on the oak tree was a woodpecker with a bright-red head that sent out messages in Morse

code. This would have made an ideal place for a stroll...
with a companion, but Dingus's mind was not on the
pleasantries the forest presented.

Moving a bit faster, the coolness of a gentle breeze
began pressing against his body. A form of air-condi-
tioning that he supposed was God's way of reasoning
with him.

Dingus moved rapidly through the woods while a
profusion of ferns made a rich, green carpet forest floor
where the inhabitants made their little secret sounds
around in the woods. At the end of his walk through
the woods, stood a black man of average height, full-
chested with rounded shoulders, well-muscled, wearing
a faded brown shirt and a pair of old, ripped overall that
partially exposed his buttocks.

Exiting the woods, Dingus approached a clear-
ing that once served as a potato field, which was now
crop-free. He thought that his sons could easily work
some of the land during their spare time, provided he
could make a deal with the owner of the field, Old Man
Morgan. He felt that it was time his two sons learned
something about the earth's soil. Dingus was a God-
fearing man. He believed one should not stray too far
from nature.

The reflection from the sun slowly moved shadows
on the ground. An azure sky was increasingly being
crowded from view by huge thunderheads that frequent-
ly hid the sun. Dingus was vaguely aware of this without

consciously giving it any particular attention as he came in sight of Aunt Phoebe's house.

Approaching the premises, he was greeted by the loud barking of dogs with the chorus of barnyard sounds, all of which prompted the appearance of a woman in her sixties dressed in a long calico dress over which she wore an apron of the same length.

The sun reflected the bones between her shoulders while the blue ribbon knotted in her hair exposed a white head of hair streaked with flecks of black. She stood beneath a large Chinaberry tree that grew in the front yard, shading her eyes with her right hand and her left hand on her hip. During the hot summers, the Chinaberry tree was a highly prized tree that was used as shade after a hard day of work in the fields.

As he approached, her face relaxed with a smile of recognition. She gracefully walked next to the wooded fence to greet her brother-in-law, passing the chicken house with rusty wire looped around the chicken house.

"Howdy, Aunt Phoebe. Hot 'nough fore you?" Dingus said, exhausted with a wiry smile.

"Yea, and more to come," she responded.

"Come in. Here's a cup for some water." Dingus had been looking forward to a fresh drink of water since finishing his lunch.

"Help yore self, and when yore done gear my horse trap. It's too hot to walk," Aunt Phoebe said, dabbing her face with a handkerchief.

There was no time for lingering around. Being a midwife was serious business, and it was an honor for Dingus to say that his brothers William, Richard, twin brother Rush, and his sister Rosie, as well as himself were ushered into the world by Aunt Phoebe.

With thin hands, the frail woman weighed less than a hundred pounds, she walked to the carriage with a satchel.

"We can get started when yore ready, Dingus," Aunt Phoebe said, before Dingus finished hitching the mule, Old Ned, to the carriage. Aunt Phoebe's custom was to waste no time in these affairs.

Loosely wrapping the reins over the footboard, he climbed aboard the carriage, he then extended his hand to grasp Aunt Phoebe's hands. It struck him how small her hands were, hands that transformed tenderness with kindness into deeds that had given hope for many families. The kind of hands one did not forget once the story they told was understood.

"Giddy up Old Ned," Dingus shouted. The carriage moved out of the yard, accompanied by a sudden peal of thunder that startled Old Ned, causing him to shy and move at a faster pace. This caused Dingus to sit stoutly at the edge of the carriage, slowing the mule to a calmer speed. The clouds closed the earth to the accompaniment of more thunder and lightning that gave worries to the native Louisianans—

Lucy had awakened slowly and in pain…there was a gentle stabbing against her kidneys. The baby was anxious to change its environments at whatever cost…The force of nature revealed its secrets bitterly. However, only a few mortal men would gladly accept pain that they believed would bring them happiness, but would only last a short time. She rose slowly out of the bed, walking into the kitchen, supporting herself with one hand on Ellen's shoulder. Ellen guided her mother around the house and quickly helped her back into the bed. Becky began whimpering, clutching onto her mother's dress.

"Brin' me a wet towel sweetie," Ellen said.

"Everythang will be alright," Lucy said, reassuring Becky.

Aunt Emma stopped by the wash shed to finish her sister Lucy's laundry.

She and Ms. Mary began chatting, which led both to carry their basket of clothes to the trail path that led to the Sweeney house. Aunt Emma and Ms. Mary entered the house to find Lucy sitting on the bed stroking Becky's head to calm her fears. "Becky brin' me a fan, and go help yore sister in the kitchen," Aunt Emma said. With this, she took command over the situation. She was comfortable with correcting her many nieces and nephews.

"Lay back, girl. Have Aunt Phoebe been sent fore?"

"Yes, she will get here," Lucy said.

The rumbling thunder could be heard far off to the eastern skies. "We could use a sprinkle," Ellen said, trying to lighten up everyone's tension.

Rosie sat on the bed next to her sister-in-law. She grimaced at Lucy's contractions.

"Ellen! Come here girl. Have you started suppa?" This put Aunt Rosie on firmer ground.

"Here, fan yore motha while I tend to the kitchen. Keep the wet towel on her head," Aunt Rosie said. She began to worry, for there was no sign of Dingus—

Dingus and Aunt Phoebe continued their journey down a muddy road where the water began to rise after a cloudburst of rain. With a sense of urgency, Dingus gave Old Ned a bit more reins. Aunt Phoebe patiently sat quietly, holding her black satchel. She knew that frustration would not calm the fickleness of nature. Dingus and Aunt Phoebe continued their ride, as the carriage began climbing up a hill. Dashing swiftly through the soak dirt road, the rain poured down heavily. The wind blew stronger as Old Ned pushed his body against the wind up the hill.

Old Ned screamed loudly, as the force from the wind lifted his four feet off the ground drifting the carriage across the dark sky, stringing the carriage across the sky as the moon became larger.

Dingus held onto the rope tighter to balance himself. Bearing not to look down below, Aunt Phoebe dug her face into Dingus's chest.

Drifting across the sky, Old Ned screamed again in excitement, and with his eyes wide open, he pushed his body against the wind. Dingus looked below.

"Oh my God, the road is flooded," Dingus said startled by the water rising. With his strength, Old Ned pushed his body against the wind. Old Ned controlled the carriage, landing it safely onto the muddy road.

The lightning became less frequent as the sound of the deep thunder rolled further east. Soon, there was a patch of sunlight glittering through the dark clouds, but the rain continued to pour down—

Waiting for her father to return home, Ellen stared out the bedroom window, counting the pattern of the hard raindrops hitting against the window. The rain drew her away from keeping the wet towel on her mother's head. "Momma, it's rainin'." Ellen felt this bit information would serve as a distraction to cheer her mother up, even to give her a slight reason to look for a bit of relief from the muggy heat. Becky heard the loud thunder that only added to her anxiety, which quickly dissipated as she saw her father and aunt riding up the road.

After assisting Aunt Phoebe off the wagon, Dingus relieved Old Ned of his burden and guided the mule beneath a huge oak tree that had grown since the Civil War. There, Dingus determined he was not needed in the house. He noticed Ellen appeared calm, but she looked exhausted.

"Come here Ellen, let's go look at the garden." She accompanied her father in the garden, as the heavenly white clouds passed the blue skies. The fresh air could be smelled for miles.

Ellen could multitask in the garden while keeping her eyes on the house. She was determined to solve the puzzle taking place in the bedroom. It took some time for Ellen and her father to walk to the garden, for it stretched some distance from the rear of the house.

"Daddy, here comes Uncle Rush and Henry," Ellen said. Although Ellen was blind, she managed to master all her five senses.

"I see you made it on time," Rush said.

"Yeah, Old Ned moves really well," Dingus sighed.

Dingus gave each of the children a different task to keep them busy.

"You kids pull some of that wet, dead grass… 'til I get back. Maybe that will keep the peace round here fore a while," Dingus said.

"I have to water Old Ned down."

"I'll fetch dinna. We all can eat dinna here," Larlue said.

"Henry, walk over to Vance's house and see if he has anything left," Dingus responded. He was referring to the weak beer Vance was famous for making—

As the family ate under the Chinaberry tree, it had become cool as twilight came.

"Phoebe has everything well in hand. Dingus let me take Ellen, Becky, and Samuel home with me for the night," Larlue suggested.

"I gues' so, Larlue," Dingus responded.

Later that night after Larlue took three of the Sweeney children home with her. Dingus and Rush walked through the woods drinking Vince's moonshine beer. The men did not pay too much attention to the bad taste, but with the authentic faith of prayer for Lucy, the two men were worried, for she had not given birth yet.

After the short walk, they both returned to the house, arming themselves with swatters.

The two men relaxed in the chairs outside the backyard, watching the onset of the night stars, accompanied by a not quite full moon.

Across a creek road that ran a mile behind their garden, there were sounds of crickets singing punctuating songs, while the bullfrogs belched "Ribbit!" songs to attract the crickets in their direction.

"Are you gonna be ordained?" Rush asked. Dingus had been considering for some time becoming a Baptist minister.

"Well, I haven' talked to Lucy about it yet. Guess I wait awhile," he responded.

"One preacher in the family is enough," Rush said with a slight smile across his face. Rush noticed an extensive look on his twin brother's face. His mind and thoughts were on more immediate concerns.

Not only was Dingus concerned of the birthing of his fifth child, but also the neighbors across the road stopping by, replenishing water from the water tap and asking, "has the baby arrived yet?"

CHAPTER 6
HAND IN GLOVE

Lucy was in labor for hours…The delivery of the baby gave Dingus discomforting thoughts that he could not put his finger on, but he remained confident for the birth of his fifth child.

Distracting his father from his train of thought, with his arms wrapped around his knees, Henry asked, "Daddy, let's go froggin', I hear some big ones."

"Not tonight, boy. Goes inside the house and get ready fore bed and don't forget to wash up. And wash more than your feet this time," Dingus said huffily. Henry's responded with his jaws grinded and tightened.

Sitting in the backyard in the dark, Dingus said a silent prayer for his wife.

"As we are now emerging from the traumatic experience of the past month, suggesting that we should pause and take a close look at ourselves, in particular, at our organization that is based on love and friendship, supposedly. These are worthy principles that go Hand in Glove, with our professed religious beliefs. The moral virtues and principles of our ancestor's humanity is that civilized man has embraced the ancestors of affection. 'Thy Kingdom of Peace on Earth'. Thus far, in spite of all of our professed beliefs and effectors, we have fallen short of the mark. We must get back to the foundation that has set civilization on its journey, the family. For with the basis of the family, there can be enough love leftover to share with our fellow human beings, for we have been blessed without fortune as those have been blessed with, thus far. Our stars express these sentiments too beautifully in their responses. For there is a passage from Adah to Electa embodying the whole notion that the greatest teacher of them all—his sole reason for leaving his throne of grace. May his love continue to shine upon us all, for that is the search for truth within us and outlives that which brings the relationship of our generations of human civilization. Amen."

It has always been a tradition for the family to celebrate the coming of a newborn infant.

With songs and poems for the well-being of a new birth, was the passage to thank God for creating life and to acknowledge the struggles of the elders and their spirits. Asking God to protect life, conserve strength, and rebuild the elder's spirits of their roots that had been lost in its antiquity. The new birth celebrated the strength, hope, will, and courage to connect with ancestors. The communication of sound, oral stories had always been handed down to celebrate the life that could be sheltered.

With oil lit lamps, there was the visiting of men, women, and children. They were slaves dressed in loose-fitted garments with worn shoes that exposed their bare feet. The women's heads were wrapped from torn clothing.

The men's heads were covered with straw hats, and the children all had dark-brown woolly hair. The tradition of generations of humanity and its antiquity is the restoring the possessions of those blessings to all people that are entitled to protect humanity and thus, His messengers sing:

The grave keeper came,
Earth and fire,
A thousand souls.

Laid with flesh.
He came quiet.

With a server;
He did not tell.
Blood He shed!

The grave keeper came;
He spared a thousand souls.

Air and wind.
No water too deep.
No soil too thick.

Hills and mountains never too high.
Blood He shed!
A thousand souls.

The grave keeper said;
He saved a thousand souls.

God's children continued their walk with their oil lit lamps across an open field into the woods.

"DADDY. It's a boooy," Henry yells. Awakened by the voice of Henry, Dingus ran to the window.

"What's the matta son?" Dingus collected his thoughts. Dingus realized he had been daydreaming.

"Good daydream?" Charles II asked.

"Yes, Father," Dingus responded.

"The Lord works in strange ways?" Charles II said.

"Yes, the Lord does," Dingus responded.

Dingus heard the strike of flesh, but there was no response. Three minutes after midnight, there was the cry of a newborn baby.

"The voice of God has spoken," Dingus cried out.

Aunt Phoebe walked out of the bedroom.

"You have to get the fire goin' again. Lucy will be just fine. It's a boy," Aunt Phoebe said tiredly.

It was July 15, 1923, the movement of time is stillness of humanity. The existence of humanity, life, and faith will equal death. After delivering the fifth Sweeney child, she asked Dingus with her frail body sitting in the rocking chair, "What's you gonna call him?"

"I likes to name him Caesar. Lucy's father...but I have to talk to her first." It became a habit for Dingus to consult with Lucy in these matters.

After such a long delivery that had put the Dingus' worries on edge, and had caused a tightening in his chest, he was unwilling to make a final decision without her support. "Cans I see her?"

"She's all yores," Aunt Phoebe said.

Walking into the bedroom, Lucy held their newborn baby.

Before, Dingus could say anything, "If it's alright with you, I likes to names him after my father?" Lucy said. With a bright smile on Dingus's face, he agreed with his wife to name their fifth child Caesar. Dingus sat next to his wife as she held Caesar snuggled in a handmade, blue quilted blanket. He held Caesar to get a clear idea of his weight, around seven pounds.

Dingus reached to touch the baby when the baby quickly grabbed his father's right index finger with his left hand, letting out a loud gurgling sound.

Holding his newborn baby son, Dingus gave Caesar a kiss on the hand that held onto his finger. "He brings us joys and hopes. He has given us a lion, the will to have courage. He will walk this earth with purpose each day. With his permission, he shall be a ruler of our weakness," Dingus acclaimed. Dingus returned Caesar to his mother, giving her a kiss on the forehead. Dingus left his wife's bedside, returning to the living room to talk about old memories with Charles II and Aunt Phoebe—

That morning he gave the children chores to do around the house and ordered Lucy to stay in bed.

It was five o'clock in the morning walking to work with Rush...and it would be the longest walk Dingus would ever take. The earth had done its fated duty and had gone to rest not consulting humanity.

The spoken words,
As I remember and recount.
There are some memories,
I can recount—

CHAPTER 7
SHREVEPORT TO CLARKS

During the plowing season the Sweeney family packed their belongings to move east; however, leaving the garden behind would be the hardest for the parents.

"Our home will be left behind. Home will always have memories...this is home. It will always be home..." Dingus said emotionally while holding Lucy's hand in comfort.

Both Dingus and Rush settled their families moving east to Clarks, Louisiana.

On arriving in Clarks, the brothers found jobs right away, working for twelve dollars and seventy cents per day. Dingus and Rush would make more money a month than they would make on a farm in a whole year. Dingus having extra money to support his family was an opportunity for his children to attend a better school. Dingus knew the children would need as much knowledge as possible.

Clarks, Louisiana was a lumber town not too far from a mining company in Alexandria, Louisiana. Fresh timber was trucked to the mill, dumped into the vast millponds, later sawed into lumber of various sizes. The cut lumber was…loaded onto flat cars to be driven to other lumbering companies.

Dingus and his brother Rush were employed at a mill company, where hard lumber was being processed into oak, birch, gum, contrary to soft lumber, such as pine. However, the lumber market began to change dramatically.

Eleven years' prior, there was a tremendous building boom following the end of World War I, and the country was recovering from its war. However, after the war, lumber became harder to sell to small companies and consumers.

October 29, 1929, the stock market crashed, creating part of the Great Depression that allowed the lumber industry to become a large exportation to corporate companies.

During this time, Dingus's talents began to show. He expressed a fine talent for carpentry and barbering. Dingus also ran a laundry business with Lucy after working a full day at the mill, and the Sweeney family became members of the Morning Star Baptist Church.

Lucy and Dingus served as ushers. Dingus later became ordained under Pastor Shorter, incorporating his own Morning Star Baptist Church—

CHAPTER 8
ASHIKO!

Grandfather Charles Sweeney II, sipping on a large cold glass of ice tea, rocking back and forth in his rocking chair, and reading the newspaper was a man with tan, brown skin. He was dressed in a complete brown man's suit. Sewed tightly to the pocket of his brown dress shirt was a large button.

A red long necktie perfectly knotted around his dress shirt, and his black shoes and shocks were fitted to perfection.

All of these clothing covered the scars on his body except his hands, exposed and swollen from his many years working as a slave in the cotton field.

Born into slavery in 1848; he had become a free black man sometime before or after the Civil War. After becoming a free black man, he taught himself how to read, write, and count; a white man taught him how to read the stock market.

Grandfather Charles II always paid attention to agriculture and the sharecropping industry, for he kept up with the prices of corn, wheat, rice.

Grandfather Charles Sweeney II lived with his son Rush and daughter-in-law Larlue. On Sundays, Grandfather Charles II always found a way to see his grandchildren. The grandchildren would stand in line waiting their turn to get a hug and a peck kiss on the cheeks from their grandfather.

Caesar always made sure he was last in line to greet his grandfather.

Grandfather Charles II read two newspapers, the *Shreveport Times* and the *Monroe Morning World*. Caesar was fond of Grandfather Charles II, as well as the special section of the newspaper.

Caesar's favorite section of the newspaper was the funnies. "Bronco Bill" and "Buck Rodgers," were his two favorite characters to read.

"Caesar, yore not into my newspaper again? I'se not finish readin'," Charles II asked.

"Caesar, come here. Sits next to yore Grandpa."

"Yeah," Caesar responded.

"Say yassuh, Caesar," his grandfather corrected him with a glare look in his eyes. He pulled Caesar by the hand to sit on his lap, "let me tell you our story."

Our ancestor's stories,
Their deep-ocean tides of history.
Our ancestor's pillar of faith,
Far away from home.

Alaba was born in 1810. Alaba's husband name was Idowu Sharma, he was born 1787. Alaba and Idowu were both from Southeast Swaziland, Africa. Alaba and Idowu had four children, Rus and Zowie twins born 1828, Dingy born 1830, and Zuberi born 1834. Alaba's daily task would be hunting for game and fishing. Alaba was always fond of swimming and fishing at Lake Nyasa.

"Object of good fishing is to tie a rope around one ankle," Alaba said, handing Zowie a long rope to tie around her mother's right ankle.

"Once I reach a certain part down in the lake, I'll pull on the rope for you to pull me up."

"How will I know if you are pulling on the rope and not the wind?" Zowie asked.

"If the rope pulls tightly you'll know it's me," she said, rubbing Zowie's shoulder, giving her daughter confidence.

"If you are in distress, yank the rope for me to swim up." Alaba and Zowie began their shop for fish at Lake Nyasa. A day of fishing would continue until the late afternoon, for Alaba and her daughter had to travel back to their village before dark.

Alaba and her husband Idowu were also crafty with handcraft baskets, utensils, and carved jewelry. When there was time of need for medicine, food, or other necessities, Alaba and her husband would trade their crafts for grain, and other crafts to survive. Their neighbors would do the same. This is how the people living in the village did business—trade crafts for food or medicine. Handcrafted baskets for oils, hand carved bowls or plates for food.

Idowu was an architect, and he would teach his sons Rus, Dingy, and Zuberi architectural skills.

He handed his son Rus a wooden knife. "Draw puzzle circles. Make the ends connect," Idowu said.

The object was the completion of ancient scribes. Idowu taught the correct way to draw designs of different shapes from circles, squares, and triangles while Dingy was in the hut weaving baskets and making medicine oils for the neighbors.

A neighbor across the way waved down Idowu. His family was in need of food. A lion had chased his wife down after hunting for game, she had caught.

"Go see my son Dingy. He will give you food," Idowu said.

"In return, I have medicine," the neighbor said—

Night had become dark and the residents in the village lit a small bonfire, entertaining each other with music, games, and handmade crafts. The village also was aware of the slave trade, for they had to be careful how and when they traveled.

"When will they return?" the neighbor asked Idowu.

"I don't know. No one tells us anything," Idowu responded.

"They take half the village on the other side of the world. Now, they move south of us. Where they take the people, we don't know," the neighbor said. Questions weighed heavily on the people's minds, as they went on with their day-by-day tasks.

Alaba and her daughter Zowie started their day early in the morning fishing on the outskirts of Lake Nyasa. A warning was given from a passerby of a slave ship on the Southwest shore of Africa. Zowie yanked on the rope for her mother to emerge to the surface of the water. Three white men were approaching the village with chains and shackles. Zowie pulled at the strap rope with force, struggling to tow her mother out of the lake.

The other women fled back to the village, warning the villagers of the slave ship. Zowie finally pulled her mother up from the waters. Her feet became tangled in the rope.

Her mother screamed, "Run, Zowie. Run!" Zowie ran back to the village warning her father and her brothers of the captors. Alaba was captured and shackled in chains with other men and women who were also fishing at Lake Nyasa.

The effort to stay free began between the Africans and the captors in the village. Idowu tried to escape with his sons and daughter, but was shot and killed.

A woman struggled with one of the captors, and was beaten down, shackled, and chained.

When the battle ended between the villagers and the captors, the men, women, and children were shackled and chained. The enslaved men, women, and children were forced to walk for miles and hours until they reached Cape Verde. Zowie saw from looking ahead that there was a mile-long stretch of men, women, and children shackled and beaten by their captors.

After several days at Cape Verde, the slaves were taken on board the slave ship and once again, the men were separated from the women.

Grandfather Charles Sweeney II reminisced, as he continued to tell Caesar of his ancestor's journey across the Atlantic.

The conditions that the enslaved men and women had endured aboard the slave ship were unimaginable, but real. The slave ship was an inhumanity that depicted the filth and smell of previous slaves who had been on the ship. The coldness and darkness, and the smell of death could be seen and felt from the slaves on the ship.

The bed cells in which they lay were inhumane, and the torturous whips the slaves suffered and endured had left them mentally incapacitated. The clacking of the chains, the smell of urine and feces, the struggle and imprint of fingernails on the walls and the floor deck of the ship would only suggest that the slaves had been fighting for their lives.

The harsh treatment of starvation and uncleanness aboard the ship was an impairment of psychological humanity that would be the traumatic suffrage of cultural identity. The slave ship traveled across the Atlantic for months. For some reason, the ship anchored at sea for several days.

An African boy, fourteen years of age solely sang the ancient drum, Ashiko. Beating drums! The slave men, women, and children from different tribes joined in Swahili tongue humbly singing:

Ashiko: Swahili Version

> Kusikia sisi Baba yetu,
> Kuja unaendelea bahari yako.
>
> wokovu wa Bwana wetu,
> Naam, tunasikia Bwana wetu,
> Coming huenda katika bahari.
>
> Katika nchi kavu,
> My Bwana Ashiko yetu kumpiga ngoma!
> Kuja unaendelea bahari yako.

Watoto wako kuzama,
Katika maji misty kama jiwe,
Mfalme wa Wafalme. Bwana wa Mabwana,
Kuja unaendelea bahari yako.

Kupumua hewa yako,
Mbinguni, huenda upepo,
Je, Bwana wetu, Ashiko kumpiga ngoma!
Unaendelea maji duniani.

Echo the Ashiko drum, the ancient culture, HEAR US OUR FATHER, OUR LORD OF SALVATION; ROLL THE WATER UPON THE EARTH. The slaves continued to sing, clamping the chains on their feet and wrists to their bed cells, the slaves sang louder. Uncontrollably the slave ship began to sail. The ship drifted, the power of the ocean tides and wind carried the ship further to the west. Unsuccessfully, the captain tried to steer the ship back on course. The cracking sounds came from the force of tides, as the ship steered off course, forcing the crewmembers to leave their post. Slave captors and crewmembers were knocked overboard drowning in the ocean…

"Captain, turn the ship around!" the slave captor yelled.

"Shut up you!" the captain shouted.

Looking through a telescope, "We're almost there. Home!" the slave captor said.

The ship approached southwest of the Gulf of Mexico. With extensive damage to the slave ship, the ship slowly floated closer to dry land.

"Those niggers destroyed our ship," the captain said heatedly.

In a low voice, "not including the deaths of men, women, and children that had drowned at sea, how many slaves did we lose, captain?"

"A hundred maybe two hundred…" the captain responded. He continued, "We can go back and get some more slaves."

Once the ship had arrived in the Americas, most likely New Orleans, Louisiana, the men, and women were separated by age. Rus and Zowie had not gotten off the ship, for Alaba thought her son and daughter were still in Africa at Cape Verde. Alaba, Dingy, and Zuberi were sold as slaves in Georgia.

However, something surprising happened some three years later, Alaba, her daughter Zowie, and her three sons Dingy, Rus, and Zuberi were together again. Alaba and her children would become slaves of Charles Sweeney.

Slave master Charles Sweeney impregnated Zowie. Zowie had a son and named him Charles II. Zowie would have a second child, a girl named Mary, by master Charles Sweeney.

It had become customary for black people who were enslaved continued naming their children after their parents and grandparents, for a form of record keeping of ancestral identity.

In the middle of the night while everyone was asleep, Zowie took her newborn daughter to a hidden area across from the slave house. She suffocated the newborn baby who was wrapped in a blanket. She struck the baby over the head with a large rock killing the newborn—

"Masta Sweeney, comes to the cabin. Zowie tooks the baby in the woods. Don't knows wha she did out there," Charles II continued, "masta was angry. I heard my motha screamin'. Masta and his wife and children and us slaves stood and watched masta Sweeney with a horsewhip to momma. He beaten her al' day and all tha' night—"

A year later, Zowie had another child named Richard from the same slave master. Grandfather Charles II recollected the memories of the inhumanity of his enslaved years.

The whippings and beatings he endured. He recounted his slave years, being shackled with chains that clinched to his wrists and ankles.

After becoming a young man, Charles II fell in love with a young woman by the name Lucie Morris, born 1860. Lucie lived on an adjoining sharecropping farm in Georgia.

With permission from slave master Charles Sweeney, Charles Sweeney II and Lucie Morris would marry in 1879. They would birth six children.

"Boy you wonda why is I tellin' you this history? I'se still sound and mind. I'se old with values. The white folk call me, intelligent nigger. God knows our internal pain and our external journey. Every day our memories, or history, our trials are all his. Always remember to thanks God, every time yore trials are tested. Always talk to the Lord, but you have to believe in Him. You have to believe in yore Lord and Savior Jesus Christ. There's three important rhythms to the beatin' drum; support, approach, and influence. Caesar, you believe in God. Do you believe in Jesus?"

"Yassuh, Granpa. I believe in the son of God." For a young boy, Caesar's words of faith would carry on in time—

CHAPTER 9

THE HEART IS UNSEEN

Years were swiftly passing, for the Sweeney family was growing fast. Caesar was curious as to the growing of his mother's stomach each month. His worries and curiosity were easy for her to see. His mother stood on the porch one morning before starting to work in her flower garden, Caesar sat on the porch watching his mother gather the tools she would need to work in her garden.

"Help me picks some tools fore the garden," Lucy said, hugged him and placed his head against her stomach.

"I will be havin' a baby soon. You'll be havin' a little brotha or sista," Lucy said with a wiry smile, stroking his curly hair.

Those simple words relieved his curiosity...

By 1935, the family had grown to eight, excluding two births in 1933. The twin sons were Earl and Frank. The first twin Earl died three days after birth and Frank survived nine months. He died in 1934. Both infants were buried near Clarks, Louisiana where Dingus pastured.

Family and friends knew Lucy as a quiet woman with a thoughtful touch. She always had a gentle smile for whomever she greeted. She had dark eyes, long jet-black hair that fell to her slim hips. Lucy always wore her skirts a hint below her knees. When she wore her hair tied up, the skirt that she wore would have a gentle flow that gave her body a flattering swing when she walked.

She inherited her almond skin from her mother Kathleen, who had been born into slavery and her mulatto features from her father, who was also mulatto and had been born a slave. The quietness of her movements and acceptance of the difficulties of her everyday existence spoke to her ancestor's blood—

There was excitement in the air. It was Sunday, church day.

Lucy prepared herself for eleven o'clock service while Dingus awakened the children for early-morning church worship. The parents proceeded with the young children to the church, walking a short distance behind. Lucy and Dingus insisted on this arrangement. Lucy had one of the few luxury items she owned, a parasol. The umbrella was a way of protecting her fair skin from the sun.

Herding the children to church, they had to walk past sharecropping land that was owned by two black families struggling with the business of farming in Louisiana.

Coming from a family that had sharecropped, Lucy was not too keen on her children becoming farmers. It had been some seventy years since the Civil War. Lucy felt that a person who continued to sharecrop was not trying hard enough to improve his or her life.

Reverend Shorter started his sermon on a positive note.

"This bright and warm Sunday mornin'…" Dingus was hoping that Reverend Shorter would keep his sermon short, for his passion ran more to politics than teaching spiritual relief.

There was the sound of a family of eight rushing in from the back entrance of the small church. Dingus, as well as worshipers, could not help but turn to the sound of the back door of the church opening. It was Henry at the age of nineteen, with six children tagging behind him, and a woman three years older than Henry.

Reverend Shorter continued his sermon, the women were cooling themselves with handmade fans, and listening to the gospel of the Lord's words.

"Yes, I remember how things used to be, but I wonder…" Dingus thought.

"Daddy was that Henry?" Ellen whispered.

"Yes sweetie. Woman and some kids." Ellen twitched her cheeks.

"But he's only nin'teen, daddy," Caesar said, sitting next to his father.

"I know son. None of those kids are his," Dingus said. The heart sometimes sees what is invisible, but there are too many boys Ellen's age around here, thought Dingus. He was bothered about the fact that Ellen had not wed yet. This thought was bringing him around to face the fact that his daughters will need to get married someday.

But still, he would hate to see his children leave home. The Sweeney children were still needed at home, especially for their mother. It would be some time before the oldest children would start their own family.

After church service, the Sweeney children, along with other children, hustled back inside the church for Sunday school.

Seizing the moment, Ellen separated from the others. Ellen and a young man sat under a Tulip Poplar tree. They flirted with words to each other and their desires for the future. She loved how the young man poked fun with her.

"Maybe you would like to come fishin' next Saturday?" he whispered in Ellen's ear. Ellen, being a practical kind, reflected the nature of her upbringing, and with few choices of words to the young man; she felt this could lead to an answer of her future.

"Well, I don't know. Mom will be goin' canning next week," Ellen said gently.

Not wanting to sound too anxious, for she did have rivals, this strategy had been used since times immemorial by women to keep men guessing. Nevertheless, it left Ellen's male companion guessing as to her intentions, accompanied by the sinking feeling that all young men would come to know. A lad's first take to seduce a young maiden was serious business, and not being able to express his true love for her.

"Will you be goin' to the annual Southern Baptist Convention?" Ellen asked. He kept his eyes focused on her blind eyes. He contended not to show his feelings for her.

"Does Old Man Wallace have any pigs to sell?" he said. Ellen felt good manners demanded that she invite the young man to stay for dinner at her parents' house.

His attention was her goal. "I don't know, but I'se ask my father if you can come over for dinna," Ellen said. Both took a desire to each other, as uninhibited young people will do.

"I know my daddy will be goin'. I'm not sure, we will be goin' to the convention for the whole five days," Ellen replied. Ever since the Sweeney family had moved to Clarks, they never missed a Southern Baptist Convention.

Attending the conferences, their mother and father meet old friends, listen to gospel hymns that they both loved, and it was a chance for Dingus to talk politics.

Standing outside, the white church, Henry noticed his father talking to some of the male church attendees. Henry introduced his wife Naomi to his father. With her having six children, four boys and two daughters, and her children would be an extension to the Sweeney name. Dingus and Naomi greeted each other with a handshake.

There was something different about Naomi, but Dingus could not put his finger on it. His curiosity of Naomi was a puzzle he could not explain that day.

Dingus's dream was for a better future for his children. He knew Henry wanted to be a builder like himself, and he hoped one-day Henry would have the opportunity to work for the Missouri Railroad Company…Hopefully, raising six children did not change his dreams for the future, for Naomi was opinionated, a controller, and her deep Southern accent and words always had suspension of doubt.

As Naomi watched her children destroy a blackberry vine, she talked about family matters with Henry,

"Well, I shores would like to see more courage from them children. I hate to see a sorry choice. George, you kids leave them berries alone. Y'all get juice all over them clean clothes," Naomi yelled.

His mind was on the price of cotton and hogs, which Ms. Mary owned as a sharecropper.

Dingus noticed all the action in progress with Naomi and her kids. He thought of the dislike of his girls leaving the nest. However, Caesar was always an observer, a good listener, and was curious about Naomi.

CHAPTER 10
AN OPINIONATED BLABBERMOUTH

The chatters of an Opinionated Blabbermouth…a bird that can quilt his way through the weakness of other people's passion in life.

This bird only has to breathe once every hour. This enables it to chirp continually without this interruption of nature. It has a tendency to prattle loudly and forcefully about things of little consequences, sly in its efforts to impress the victims of its good intentions and kindness, thereby installing in the mind of its victims its harmlessness. There may be a small advantage, but on close inspections, the advantage is small indeed.

Repayment will be expected, even demanded. Of course, the more of these small favors accepted, the larger the debt becomes. On closer examination of the blabbermouth's motivation of habits, one can protect one's self from this bird, and deal with it more effectively.

The prime weakness of the blabbermouth is prison, gambling, and distorting the truth or outright lying. It is an expert at playing on the sympathy of its intended victims, getting the matter-of-fact done for itself.

It has an enormous greed for money, although it does not understand the basic laws of finances, only in the sense where it is applied to pleasure.

The opinionated depends upon its victim's innocence and desires, thereby blinding it to its true motive. Given this advantage, it can present its shortcomings as qualities; even encourage its victims to practice them also, a very dangerous thing. The best and most proven method in dealing with the opinionated blabbermouth is when in its presence. Say little and make no promises or commitments.

This bird does not discriminate in selecting its victims, male, female, relatives, or strangers.

Although it prefers strangers, age does not matter when selecting its intended prey. In some ways, the blabbermouth can be compared to the black widow spider. The spider may get through to its victim in a matter of minutes. This may take months, even years in subduing its prey.

The opinionated blabbermouth has freeloading tendencies when it comes to providing shelter for themselves, depending mostly on others for this necessity. Its expertise lies in the pursuit of pleasure. The blabbermouth is endowed with certain virtues that it fits impose upon it. Those that cannot escape and are claimed to be self-imposed by this bird, and with a bit of hocus-pocus the unwary victim is taken in. As a rule, the opinionated avoids being known as an outright liar and a sneaky controller, this it does only in extreme instances of secrecy—deceit and the subtle bending of truth is its style, if skillfully applied.

Beware when dealing with this bird; thus forewarned!

CHAPTER 11
SURVIVING THE GREAT DEPRESSION

During the winter of 1935, the effects of the Great Depression had considerable impacts on international trade, the lumber industry, and its effect on families were particularly severe.

The father was known by neighbors as a strict father, but he was also a caring man. He works long hours to provide for his family, and expected the same from the children when they grew to be adults.

Dingus was a deeply religious man, and he forbid such games such as cards, dominoes, and dice around the house. The father allowed the children to play checkers at home. Lucy only allowed card games and dominoes, believing that card games and dominoes would help the children to learn how to calculate faster.

She was right!

Out of respect for Dingus' wishes, such games would be put away before he came home from the hard mill. On Sundays, Dingus would give his sermons at the local schoolhouse. The tithes and offering went back to help the Clarks community. Yet, the family continued to struggle. On Thursdays, Dingus would come home from work to attend to his other job that he was instrumental in establishing, a lodge called the Free and Accepted Masons in Clarks, Louisiana.

"Caesar, you don't wanna to listen to these girls argue all day. Come goes with me," Dingus said.

Caesar was happy to see that his father was letting him attend a Free and Accepted Masons meeting held at the schoolhouse.

Walking to the schoolhouse with his father, Caesar reflected on the hardship of the Great Depression. Wintertime was one of the hardest seasons to escape from the stress of the Depression. He thought about how cold it would be walking to and from school with thin clothing to wear and little food to eat.

The night before school, his mother would bake potatoes in her old oven. His mother would give each child a potato to put in their coat pocket, hence the children could stay warm while at school.

At school, Caesar's brothers and sisters would have a snack to eat and when coming home for lunch, there would be a slice of crumbed bread...

Lucy would promise her children that they would come home to a full meal after school, for the Great Depression took a toll on the Sweeney's finances and other families across the country.

Arriving at the schoolhouse, Dingus and Caesar walked up a flight of stairs that led them to a classroom. The door was locked. Dingus unlocked and opened the door with a key that he had tucked in his overall pocket. Caesar watched his father set up the room, not knowing what to expect, and poked around the room, while Dingus pulled out different color cloths from a cardboard box.

The room stood internally bright by itself with four walls and smoky thick paint meek with salvation. A single window frame was mounted to the oak wood with perfection, clearly to be treasured with white snow that had covered the corners of the outside frame of the window.

The salvage chairs and a large desk weighed heavy. All stood with column legs. Standing in front of the chairs and desk, nailed in four places to a podium was a cross.

Caesar discovered that the room only held some blue and white aprons and white collars, along with some furniture that the school never used. He was disappointed;

however, the mystery of the meetings deepened his curiosity.

His father set up the table and the room to his satisfaction.

"Time fore you to leave the room. Sits on the steps outside. Don't walk off anywhere," Dingus said.

Members of the Free and Accepted Masons began arriving at the schoolhouse. Each member had to know the passcode knock to enter the lodge room. Caesar tried to memorize the lodge member's door knock. However, the last member door knock was longer than the other members knock at the door. With his ears glued to the door, he was unable to hear a sound within the room.

When the masons meeting ended, the men went home to their families. Caesar and his father returned home sometime before midnight.

"Time fore bed son. Yore a fast learner, boy. Don't think I didn't see you learning those passage knocks," Dingus continued, "wash up an' change in yore long johns, son," added his father. Caesar obeyed his father's orders and slipped into bed. Dingus left the bedroom door cracked open and Caesar saw his father sitting behind a wooden desk he had made two years ago, writing in a journal.

The journal had been passed on to Dingus from his father Charles II. Written in the journal were sharecropped prices of goods and services. The price of hogs, bales, goods that were bought and sold, and a Parish tax in Richmond, Louisiana by Dingus and Charles II.

The journal also included his father's ministry that he had formed, the Morning Star Baptist Church in Clarks, Louisiana. The journal entries were records of member names, tithes, and offering.

CHAPTER 12

RAZOR STRAP

In the spring of 1936, Dingus wed off his daughter Ellen. Becky moved out of the house and began having relations with men. Five children were left in the Sweeney family.

The children's names were Samuel, age fifteen, Caesar, age thirteen, Matthew, age ten, Sarah, age eight, and Stella, age four.

Caesar and his sister Becky argued a lot over little things. Being one of the oldest siblings, Becky always tried to out-boss him, but was never successful. She knew for a fact that their parents had chosen Caesar to rule the Sweeney family. Although he was younger than Becky, their father wanted a strong hand and strong mind in the family.

Dingus went to work at the hard mill on a Sunday morning. While Dingus was at work, Lucy baked a batch of tea cookies for Sunday's service. Lucy placed the cookies in a glass jar that Dingus had bought her for Mother's Day.

After covering the tea cookies with a clean white cloth, she went to visit her sister-in-law Rosie that lived across the way from the family house. Having a sweet tooth, Caesar and Matthew had gotten into the tea cookies. After leaving the house, their mother noticed that the screen door was not how she had left it.

"Those two rascals gotten into my tea cookies, again," Lucy said to Rosie.

Later, that day after Dingus had a rough day working at the hard mill, and ministering at the Morning Star Baptist Church, the family sat at the dinner table waiting for Lucy to serve dinner. After dinner, Lucy and Dingus went outside, updating each other about current events... and the children. Lucy expressed her concern about Caesar and his brother Matthew, because they both had eaten all the tea cookies.

Knowing what was to come next, Caesar and Matthew went to the outhouse to protect themselves from their father's whippings. Caesar had unbuttoned the hatch part of Matthew's overalls, covering his hide with some newspaper. Matthew did the same for Caesar, placing some newspaper down in his overalls, smoothing the newspaper...

"Did you smooths out the newspaper good," Matthew asked.

"I'se don't thinks daddy will notice…" Caesar laughed, double checking the smoothness of the newspaper that covered his buttocks.

When their father was tired after a hard day at work, he would use his razor strap.

"CAESAR. MATTHEW. COME INSIDE."

They both walked into the house with angel faces. "CAESAR. GO GET MY RAZOR STRAP," their father said impatiently.

Caesar walked to his desk and pick up the razor. He shyly handed his father the razor strap. Dingus leaned him over his legs to give him a whipping for getting into the tea cookies.

POW! The neighbors could hear a loud hollow sound coming from the Sweeney house.

Dingus pushed Caesar off his legs quickly with surprise and guilt. Lucy and Dingus walked to their bedroom, when sounds of scuffling started coming from their bedroom.

Caesar went to investigate the scuffling sounds in his parent's bedroom. He peaked into the bedroom, and there; his parents were laughing their hearts out. Caesar outsmarted his father's strenuous whipping.

CHAPTER 13

FAITH

A June storm was approaching Louisiana that had created massive damages to homes and businesses in Texas.

Larlue and Naomi were visiting Lucy, reminiscing over old times. Larlue realize she had left her pink, pagoda-shaped umbrella back at her house. Instead of having one of Naomi's children fetch her umbrella, she chose Caesar to recover her umbrella...five minutes away from his house. He dashed out the front door, pushing his body against the strong wind that pounded his dark skin across the large field.

The dark sky covered the light from the moon that made it hard for him to see.

Caesar saw a light flickering across the open field; he was seconds away from Aunt Larlue's house and it was hard for him to see what was in front. He tripped over a stump, landing on his left rib cage.

His head had landed on some boulder rocks. His body soaked in the puddle of mud and blood, as the spirit lifted his body, Caesar closed his eyes. A piercing light glazed across the sky.

He stood frozen in front of the light, as it brushed his body.

A spectacle of light encompassed his body. The warmth, stillness, and refuge were dissolution, and sense and awareness.

The intense feeling of unconditional love and acceptance was well-being and painlessness. Caesar saw himself happy, running cross an open field.

A hand motioned for him to stop.

"Turn back around. Turn back around," the voice of a man said. Galloping on horses through a heavy storm across an open field were three cowboys heading west. Their horses screamed from the sudden bright light. Sitting deep in their saddles the three men halted their horses.

"Did y'all see that?" a black man name Hoppie said.

"Nothin' but both you and Frank's bright lights shining in my face," a white man named Bobby said.

"I thought I told you both to turn off your gas lamps," Bobby screamed loudly, while the pouring rain pounded his face as he tried to think of the correct direction of travel.

"Wasn't our lamps," a white man name Frank said.

Bobby's horse whinnied and grunted.

"Look over there, Frank! A pools of blood and mud," Hoppie said.

"Heavens to Betsy!" Bobby said franticly holding the rope slightly on his horse's neck.

"We ain't gonna leave this boy here, are we?" Hoppie asked.

The rain poured down heavy, the three men carefully uncovered Caesar's injured body soaked in mud and water.

Bobby sprung upward onto his saddled horse while Frank carried Caesar, carefully sitting him in front of Bobby. Hoppie tied a rope to the ring of the halter to lead the horse. The three men carefully galloped east through the storm to a hospital located in Winnsboro.

"Hah. H-yah," with urgency, the three cowboys rode on their horses through the cracking thunder and rain.

Bobby carried Caesar's injured body into the emergency room.

"We found this boy injured some thirty miles from here," Frank said.

"Never heard of 'Some Thirty Miles.' We're not taking any more patients. Doctor's busy," a white female nurse with a snarly look on her face said.

"This boy injured. The boy is bleeding to death. Look at him," Frank said. She gave the three men a blank stare.

"Wait here..." The nurse returned back from consulting with the doctor, "Y'all can't leave without paying. Hospital rules," she said hesitantly. Hoppie glared at her, knowing otherwise. Hospital rules.

The three men gathered up what money they had to admit Caesar into the hospital.

"You cowboys can leave. There's a saloon not too far from here," she said.

"Miss, we ain't leaving until doc fixes this boy," Bobby said.

The doctor requested for the three men, after a couple of hours in the emergency room...

"You cowboys know this boy?" the doctor asked.

"No, sir. Found him thirty miles back in. Is he gonna make it doc?" Bobby asked. The doctor nodded his head. A few more minutes of silence passed, and Bobby realized he was crying.

"What's your name, boy?" Bobby asked, softly.

"Caesar Sweeney." He had a mild case of amnesia.

"We'll find your folks."

"I'll stay with the boy," Frank said.

"I'll ride back where the cattle are and let Johnny know what has happened," Hoppie said.

"Tell Johnny to come to the hospital if we're not all back at the post in two days," Bobby said.

CHAPTER 14
THE SEARCH

"Hoppie, don't you feel right about now...the world is empty?" Bobby asked.

"More so, Bobby," Hoppie replied.

"It's been three days. No sign of his family. Let's camp here tonight and get an early start in the morning," Bobby said.

The beautiful nature trail guarded by the scent of the breezy air floras in the woods'...and as the sun began to settle in the west, Bobby and Hoppie began to settle down their camp site not too far south of Clarks.

"That hurricane was a violent one...Twisted our direction...Bobby," Hoppie said.

"I wouldn't wish a hurricane like that on no state..." Bobby responded.

Along with a pot of coffee hanging over a tin camp-fire stove were two rabbits rotissering that had been caught earlier that day. In fact, the discussion of searching for Caesar's family allowed Bobby and Hoppie to pause and reminisce...

"I remember seeing a trestle, where we had found the boy. A sign... 'Dead Man Curve'," Bobby recalled.

"Come to... 'Dead Man Curve'. A trestle. Wuz tha?" Hoppie asked.

"I don't know about a puddle of blood. But, a trestle. You know, an A-shape frame used as a barrier. Some mill companies used them to stack plywood on to saw," Bobby responded.

"You saw all that...in the dark? If you say so, boss," Hoppie said, sipping on his cup of coffee. Bobby and Hoppie turned in for the night, hoping for better luck the next day in searching for the Sweeney family.

The next morning, the two men made and ate breakfast. After breakfast, Bobby and Hoppie saddled up both their horses, heading west through the deep woods.

A trestle was spotted, but no sign of any company mill. Not too far in an open field was a stump covered in dry mud and twigs, and houses hidden between tall trees and bushes.

A black man with a black mustache and thick pepper hair approached the two men.

"Howdy sir," Bobby and Hoppie greeted the black man,

"My partner and I are looking for the parents of a young negro boy," Bobby said.

"A young negro boy!" repeated the black man.

"Yessir. Missing a child?" Hoppie asked, without giving away the description of Caesar.

"Dingus Sweeney. My son's name is Caesar Sweeney. We live in the Company house," Dingus pointed to the trees and bushes that hid the houses.

"Cans you take me and my wife to our son? Our mule is lame. We have a carriage to take us to Winnsboro," Dingus asked humbly.

Bobby and Hoppie guided their horses to the carriage to be harnessed. Hoppie stood left of each horse holding the horses by the bridle. Bobby slid the shafts through the tub loops on each side of the horses. He adjusted the tugs, attached the tugs to the carriage threading them between the girth and belly band. He attached clips at the end of the tugs onto the carriage.

Hoppie tighten the girth, checked the straps making sure the tugs were not twisted.

Bobbie grasped the reins not letting go. The horse-drawn carriage carrying the four made its way traveling slowly east, towards the hospital in Winnsboro, a small town.

Lucy ran to her son's bedside weeping. "You'll gonna be alright, baby," Lucy cried, tears swelling down her face. Dingus held and rubbed the soft tenderness of his son's hands. Lucy examined his body searching for injuries, patting his torso with her hands.

Dingus turned to two the three cowboys and explained that "I'se doesn't hav' much money. I have hogs, coffee, sugar, oats, ask fore Matthew," he said.

"We don't want anything from you folks. We all will pray for your son," Bobby responded.

"A prayer is what we all need," Hoppie directed to Dingus... "And not only so, but we glory in tribulations s also' knowing that tribulation worketh patience; And patience, experience; and experience, hope; and hope maketh not ashamed; because the love of God is shed abroad in our hearts by the Holy Ghost, which is given unto us."

—Romans 5:3-5.

Dingus, Lucy, and the three cowboys prayed at Caesar's bedside. The three cowboys left his beside. Dingus and Lucy exchanged sincere gratitude of good to the three cowboys—

Bobby and Hoppie galloped fast down the dusty road on their horses, for a storm was approaching the small city of Winnsboro.

CHAPTER 15

THE TRAVEL

It was late June 1936, when Caesar awakened from his accident. Leaning over him with a shiny stainless steel stethoscope stood a doctor pressing against his chest, trying to hear his heart beat. His accident was a life and death recovery, and the doctors at the hospital could do only little for Caesar.

The accident had paralyzed the left side of his body with fractured ribs. A doctor in training, told him of a better hospital his parents should consider. For the doctors, at Winnsboro Hospital did not have the medical experience to treat his fractured lungs and ribs.

Upon his parents' visit, Caesar mentioned of a better hospital called Charity Hospital.

"…They couldn't do no worse," Lucy said continued, "why don't we let him try Charity Hospital."

"I don't know about this…Will he be healed. All these doctors are doin' in pushing medicine down his throat and he continue to ill. Will those doctors at Charity Hospital take care of our son?" Dingus responded, his fists tightens. However, this may be; it is the approach, or rationale, of process and progress from thought, with matters of all that a solution to revive and protect the health of their son was critical.

Caesar parents decided to discharge him from the hospital, for they wanted to take care of him and with home remedies. Caesar would slowly recover from his accident. He was put on a strict diet that included eggs, fish, meats, and vegetables to help strengthen his body.

However, Lucy and Dingus knew their son needed more than home remedies; he needed a doctor. In the winter of 1936, Caesar was admitted to Charity Hospital.

Standing beside his bed stood a doctor that spoke with a heavy German accent. Because of the doctor's strong heavy accent, Caesar could not understand some of the words the doctor was speaking. "Don't worry, I'll take care of you. Family, friends?" the German doctor questioned.

Caesar felt a sharp pain in the left side of his body.

"Don't move. Don't move," the doctor said.

Death then life, Caesar clearly remembered.

The force of a hand had guided him away from the light, a person that would not reveal his face. Caesar was guided away from a whirl funnel light.

The doctor concluded that he would need a series of operations. The first two operations were the removal of one of his left ribs.

After recovering from the two operations, Charity Hospital allow Caesar to travel home to be with his family.

"Dingus we've don't have enough money fore Caesar to travel home. I don't want him gettin' on that train or bus," Lucy said, concerned for her ill son having to ride on the train and being exposed to racism.

"I think he be alright. He knows how to greet them white folks," Dingus said.

Charity Hospital had a high-quality reputation for their medical staffed doctors, and part of Charity Hospital services was providing transportation for patients who could not afford to pay for hospital services.

Caesar's transportation to and from home was paid by Charity Hospital. He traveled from the hospital to go home by train, where his mother would be waiting for him in front of fabric shop in Clarks. The train made a brief stop near Clarks, Louisiana. Sitting in the back of the train, Caesar looked out the window to see his mother giving him an excited wave. Caesar slowly lifted himself up from the seat to walk toward the entrance to the train. His mother stood at the entrance of the train and helped him walk down the stairs. A man standing behind him carried the wheelchair off the train.

"Thank you," Lucy said.

"You're welcome," the black man responded.

"Caesar, you ready to go home?" Lucy asked, smiling while placing her hands on his face.

"Yes, ma'am, cans we stop at the candy store?" Caesar asked excitedly. With a gentle smile, she pushed the wheelchair to the candy store located not too far from the train station.

Caesar picked out his favorite candy, pointing out to the clerk the 'Fireballs' that sat freshly in a glass jar. After paying for the candy, Lucy wheeled him home. However, his visit with his family would only last a couple of days, for the doctors wanted to monitor Caesar's recovery.

Lucy would clean the operation wounds, sometimes reopening the stitches making sure the operation wound was cleaned thoroughly.

Because of the severe condition of his lungs, Caesar was unable to breathe on his own. Doctors had to insert a tube in his mouth that had to pass through his vocal cords. This gave a passage way for his lungs to stay open and for him to breathe. Caesar was only allowed to eat very little foods because of the tube.

There were times when the endotracheal tube would cause an infection in his lungs.

CHAPTER 16
FIRST SUNDAY CHURCH SERMON

"We receive Him in the name of Christ Jesus, the son of God, and the seed of David. It is a pleasure to be standing in front of you all today in the House of the Lord to worship His victories. The work of God, our Lord and Savior Jesus Christ, we all have inherited his strength and because of Jesus' bravery and his will. Today, we cannot fail the Lord, our ancestors, and we cannot fail our second ancestors. To walk the face of the earth each day, as people of all creeds, colors, and races, we cannot fail God," Dingus said, as sweat profusely rolled down his face.

"We haven't witnessed each other's pain, trials, and suffering because we have not accepted our own trials and thanked God faithfully for lifting us up, when we have fallen down. Today, I speak on our Father, his trials, his strengths, and his victories. God is our soul. When we fall down, He is our victory when we get right back up and worship him," Dingus wiped the sweat from his face and continued, "when the devil pulls the wool over our eyes with his trickery and illusions, the first thing we must do is turn to the Lord. He will bring us back to reality. Evil is spiteful, evil is the opinionated blabbermouth, the I'm A 'Gonna Bird. Evil is faithless. When we want it quick, short, fast, and easy, these are not the Lord's victories. Because the Lord always brings his children back to reality, he will send his counselors to his suffering children. With strength, we trust the Lord, the highest Father of them all. For Jesus was never weak from his challenges. Our Lord and Savior Christ Jesus walked life with determination and with skills. He gave his life so that we would be free from our sins. He paid the ultimate price to save us from our sins. With all that he has paid, we give him the Hand in Glove. He was crucified; and he risen on the third day and walked the face of the earth. He took beatings for his good words, yet he was crucified," Dingus said, his black robe soaked the sweat from his body. He continued to facilitate encouragement to his congregation. "The Lord's strength is a bright light; he will show you his spirit is true. But, you have to believe in God. You have to believe in Jesus Christ. You have to accept Christ as your Savior. However, we must have followers so that they can become leaders. You can confine yourself to selfishness or you can expand your life to do the good work of God without limitations. Because God created order, He created simple rules for those of us who truly believe in his words and follow these orders in the way things are supposed to be," he continued to preach, his body becoming limp and tired. However, the strength of speaking Jesus' name, lifted his grace to continue with the victory.

"I ask that our time be to walk with Jesus, closely in our life. It's hard for us to do things right when we have been doing wrong and we continue to do wrong because we know how to do right. Our hope is in God because we are his children. He purifies our hearts and to make us more like Him each day. I submit each day to God, let us all rejoice and be glad that God would help us to be that kind of friend who is sure to help in times of trouble. We shall turn to the Lord, the solid rock on which we all stand and ask God to lead us the way we should go and help us to always live in faith of Him. He builds castles," Dingus said, lifting his hands up to the sky.

"God's power and ability is to do the impossible and He helps us to be a person who brings the good news of His salvation to others. Put your trust in God. He hears our prayers. God will lead his suffering children, saving his work for our good, because paths will appear when we draw ourselves closer to God.

He will help give you strength to face all life's challenges. The Lord will give us strength. Our will always be victorious. I ask that if you are a true believer in Christ and you want to draw yourself closer to your Lord and Savior come forward. Our journey may be a thousand miles, but our faith in him is right in our souls. He is a leader of strength. He is the victory of all our challenges," Dingus said, lifting his hands, the congregation stood to their feet, wailing with joy and conviction.

"I say to you, join our heavenly Father who gave up the ghost for our sins. Walk with our Lord and Savior Jesus Christ. Let the blood pass through and walk with faith. Walk with strength. Walk and join Jesus your heavenly Father to his victory," Dingus' said, his voice brittle and hoarse from his determination to teach the truth of grace.

The congregation of all saved people, men, women, children, and elders, walked through the woods to Blackfoot River singing in victory.

They walked where red vines branched and the harmony of fallen leaves and thin branches cracked while landing on the uneven ground. The insects hummed while the birds sang. There was the sweet, wood smell of ferns, plants, and the lovely fresh smell of lemon Queen Flowers Sunflowers:

Walk with Jesus,
To Calvary,
On the highest mountain.

I walk with Jesus,
The highest healer,
To victory.

I say,
Walk with Jesus,
Our amazing King,
To Calvary cross.

Walk with Jesus,
The rock. The mighty King.
Who gave up the ghost,
I walk with Him.

Sunlight freely strength,
Water sweet and glassy,
Harmony of joy and blessing.

I sing the Lord's Victory.
I say.

I walk with Jesus,
Our mighty Savior,
Authentic from hunger and thirst.

Jesus healing power;
He the saving power;
He owns our victories,
Yea, I walk with Him.

Crossing a flat wooded bridge, the people continued to sing in the sweet earthy air, as the sunlight filtered through sugar maple trees as they changed from yellow to orange to red. The shafts of light clustered between the trees while the shifting patterns of the trees became taller. The breeze stirred. Overhead, the woods opened. The sunlight reached Blackfoot River, the sun's silhouette mounted the river.

In a white gown, Caesar pushed his weak body to walk with his family and the congregation through the woods. He became stronger as he continued to walk to the river. He was a true believer.

Becky tripped and fell, landing on her knees, Naomi ran to Becky's fall and helped her back to her feet. Becky and Naomi found themselves not singing the victory. Their voices were silent.

Dingus stood in the river ministering in his white gown. With his arms extended, he stretched his arms out for Caesar to walk in the river to receive the Holy Ghost.

He placed his left hand over his nose, supporting his son's back with his right hand, he said, "I now baptize you Caesar Sweeney in the name of the Father, the Son, and Holy Ghost. Buried with Jesus Christ in the likeness of His death, and rose with Him in the likeness of His resurrection to walk in the newness of life. Amen."

CHAPTER 17
HOME AFTER COMMUNION

The first Sunday, after communion that evening, the sun filtered the skies longer than usual.

Dingus handed Caesar his grandfather's journal and a picture of his grandfather. He also handed him a picture of his mother's great-aunt and great-uncle, and a tintype photo of his African ancestor Zuberi. Caesar faithfully held on to the inheritance memorabilia.

He placed the memorabilia of his ancestor's history in a brown pillowcase his mother made for him.

"…I have dinna ready fore you, dear," Lucy said. Dingus gave his son a hug. He left his bedside for Lucy to be alone with her son.

"Momma, what's this," Caesar asked, pulling a piece of paper that was folded with a picture his father had given him.

Lucy glared at the folded paper. She slowly opened the letter "this is when I was a child," she said.

"What's it say? The letter is written in a column of words." Lucy massaged her neck thinking of what to tell her son.

"These words are written in codes," Lucy answered and continued "this is what it says," she said, pointing to the letters and outlining the words with a pencil.

Lucy could not resist, but to show her son how to read and write in letter codes. She left her son, for he became occupied practicing how to write letter codes.

Up the road, neighbors could hear Naomi arguing with Henry. The fall hot weather brought out the heated drama that evening, as neighbors stood outside their front yard listening to the argument. The argument made its way to the Sweeney's house, where stood a young boy in the middle of road playing with some twigs.

"Ooh, yore in trouble. Lady the boss," a nine years old boy said, directing his comment to Henry.

Dingus stood on the front porch that led to the inside of the house.

"Good evenin' Naomi," Dingus gestured.

"Talks to yore son—Puttin' his hands on my children will be the last thing he does in my house—Talks to yore son," Naomi said, ignoring Dingus, walking into the Sweeney house.

Folding clothes in the living room, Lucy and Becky became distracted from the argument between Naomi and Henry. The younger Sweeney children stood next to their father.

Dingus removed his straw hat. He patiently ordered the children to leave the house.

"Baby, bring me a hot cup of coffee," Dingus said. Taking his first sip of hot coffee, he finally reached his point of patience to end the argument.

"Everyone. Leave the room. Now. That includes you, Henry. Caesar, stay in bed," Dingus yelled.

"I don't know from what ship you anchored off, buts you're not gonna to talk me like you talk to my son in my own home. Those children's of yores is spoiled brats. My son works, he feeds those tar pit kids of yours. Henry puts clothes on those children's backs," Dingus said, sipping on freshly made brew coffee, he said, "yes, I tore into some of yore children's asses fore destroying my wife's garden. And you don't even know how to take care of those snotty nose kids of yores," Dingus calmly distracted how Naomi was becoming a distraction to the Sweeney family affairs, family close relationship, and family values.

"My wife cleans their dirty, nasty snots when you bring them down here to the house. A cat with no litter box," Dingus said, taking another sip of his coffee.

"I hear you told my daughters, they could be western women. Havin' them playin' with those blue saloon feathers."

"Yore daughters will soon be steppin' out into the real world. They need some street wisin'," Naomi said.

"I have five sons, and four daughters. My daughters don't wear makeup. Yore not gonna turn my daughters into 'ladies of the night', like yourself. You don't even have a pot to piss in and a window to throw it out. Yore poison and yore a disgrace to my son and my family. As long as I'm livin', yore not gonna turn my family into poison spiders. And you betta not put my son six feet under like you did your last two husbands. Next time yore children get into my wife's garden it ain't gonna be a twig landin' on their asses," Dingus continued, "I thought you learned something today in communion. You have a blessed day," he muttered, comfortably sitting in his wife's rocking chair. Naomi hefted herself up from the couch. The color red covered the brown skin of a black woman. Dingus was now convinced that black people's faces can turn red.

"Communion and now trouble. Can't believe it, us Negroes do turns red," Rush muttered. However, one would have to see it to believe it.

"Caesar, gets ready fore me to give you a bath, before you go back to Charity Hospital tomorrow. Don't forget to say yore prayers," Dingus reminded his son, standing in the doorway to the boy's bedroom. Not knowing

87

that his father had been standing there, Caesar's ears had been glued to the wall listening to every detail word coming from his father.

CHAPTER 18
READY FOR WORK

August of 1937, Caesar returned home after spending a year at Charity Hospital. He was behind in
his schooling. Lucy found a job as a cook, working for
a politician in Clarks, Louisiana. She birthed her last
child, Adam in 1937. Caesar had taken ill with bronchitis a month after he had been discharged from the
hospital and was again admitted at Charity Hospital to
receive bronchitis treatments.

In the winter of 1937, the father worked odd jobs to
make extra money; for that he could buy the materials
needed to make Caesar a new pair of shoes. Dingus did
not want his son to miss any more school because he was
a year behind...

Two days before Christmas, Dingus had taken ill
with pneumonia, and he continued to ail the following

year of 1938. Lucy and Caesar stayed at home to nurse
Dingus.

"Caesar come here next to yore father. Sing with
me."

The sluggard does plow,
When will He hear?
The faith do I have,
When will He see?

The bread that I eat,
When will He come?

The rock.
The spirit.
I am too blind to see.

Journey and opinion,
Survival of my journey,
Treasure and death,
Shall man revile and persecute me.

My daily trials,
Why do I suffer?
My daily challenges,
Why do I stumble?

The judge I am patient,
He wins my victories.

The rock.
The spirit.
I am too blind to see.

He the King of Kings.
He the Lord of Lords.
He's my beating drum,
I now see.

Long days and nights, Lucy and Caesar stayed by
Dingus's bedside, comforting his ailing soul and lifting
his spirit with good memories. Lucy saw the tiredness in
Caesar's eyes.

"Baby goes and lay down. I watch your father," she
said. Caesar walked to his bedroom shivering from the
thin clothes that covered his body.

Dingus spirit came to Caesar, as he gazed outside
the bedroom window, the cold winter air numbed his
body.

"I want you to let go of yore fears. God decides whom
lives and who dies. Send your message to the Lord. He
will hear you. Ask the Lord to spare your life, for what
reason? Faith will stop when you stop believing in faith.

Don't jeopardize your faith in Christ who is in God. I'm going away, but promise me you will always obey your mother and never do anything that would bring her shame. Let go of all your doubts and be strong to live, to want, to have what God is giving you. Don't let God go. God is the only 'one-time keeper'. Any man who says he is a timekeeper is a fool. Sometimes son, we have to let go of our brothers and sisters. It's called tough love. You will be faced with battles with your brothers and sisters. Help you brothers and sisters all that you can, but don't fall into their trickery and illusions. You can only help them for so long. If you must, let them go," Dingus said, his spirit soon disappeared.

Lucy screamed!

Dingus Sweeney was a tall man with flecks of gray hair, jet-black mustache, and medium brown skin. He was a slender built, powerful man. Dressed proudly in his blue overalls and jumpers, a light, blue shirt, and heavy working shoes, and always had a "chaw" of tobacco in his jaw. His thumbs hooked into his suspenders where they fastened onto the bib of his overalls, standing tall. Then again, he always looked handsome in his black blazer jacket, white shirt, black tie, black pants, and his black patent leather shoes that he kept polished to an eye-dazzling shine.

Ready for work!

Morning Star Baptist Church was the house of the birth, life, and worshiping that the Sweeney family came to love after moving from Shreveport. In an open casket rested a father, a preacher, and a Free and Accepted Mason.

CHAPTER 19
A TOWER OF STRENGTH

"Hadn't my father been given a fair price, for his products as a sharecropper, could he have been a more prosperous farmer than he was?"

Eulogy

I celebrate my victory,
Yesterday, I cried a river,
With my trials and error,
The Lord was there to lift me up.

Yesterday, I could not breathe silently,
With all my worries,
The Lord was there.

Yesterday, I cried a rapid sea,
With all my stumbles,
But God was there to guide me to salvation.

Yesterday, I was a fighter of all my trials.
With all my struggles, and efforts,
He gave me more strength and
I am still a fighter.

A tower of strength,
The glory of my victory.

My journey may had been short,
But today, I celebrate my new life, because
Yesterday is gone,
Today, I celebrate my life with victory.

⋙ ⋘

To: Dingus Sweeney

"I have fought the good fight, I have finished my course, I have kept the faith: Henceforth there is laid up for me a crown of righteousness, which the Lord, the righteous judge, shall give me at that day: and not to me only, but unto to all them also that love his appearing."

—II Tim 4:7-8.

Charles II and Lucie Sweeney were blessed with the birth of their son Dingus, he came into this world March 15, 1896, the second of six children, and Christ graced his life at the age of nine. In 1913, Dingus and his twin brother Rush moved to Georgia where they farmed not too far from the Bonner farm. There he met Lucy. This happy occasion occurred on April 1914. From this union came eleven children, seven boys, and four girls.

Six years after their marriage, they moved to Clarks, Louisiana, and being Christian and brought up in the Christian way; they rejoined as members of Morning Star Baptist Church, and where he had become ordained. Dingus's dream was to build houses, cabinets, and furniture, and he formed an organization the Free and Accepted Masons. His life was filled with a pillar of strength and courage. Growing up in poverty, he worked on a plantation farm with his parents not too far from the Bonner farm.

Becoming an adult, as a farmer he struggled to survive in the farming industry. He worked for the Company in Shreveport...later moving to Clarks where he was employed at the mill. He was an entrepreneur, a barber, an architect, and a preacher. He now joins his brother William, his father Charles II, and his mother Lucie. The passage written by the apostle, Paul, in II Timothy 4:7 says, "I have fought a good fight, I have finished my course, I have kept the faith."

A progressive man he was, as an asset to his country and denied the birthright to his country, for Dingus Sweeney died at the age of forty-three.

He died in January 1938. He leaves behind his wife Lucy, and nine children, Ellen, Becky, Henry, Samuel, Caesar, Matthew, Sarah, Stella, and Adam, his twin brother Rush, his brother Richard, and his sisters Rosie and Estella. Two sons-in-law, two daughters-in-law, and one brother-in-law, cousins, and uncles, nephews and nieces."

Caesar could only wonder about what could have been or what should have been for his father.

He could not help noticing his siblings were sitting in the back of the church while his mother, his uncles, aunts, and cousins sat toward the front of the church.

Aunt Emma sat next to Caesar in the first row in the church. She whispered in his ear, "Yore brothers and sisters are afraid of dead people."

Dead people!

He thought when the spirit is separated from the human body, the spirit is released to the earth, finding its way to Heaven. Depending on how many hard knocks one has to walk through, there are doors to enter in order for the body to be fully renewed. The message of trouble and stress will be for those to rest, a sanctuary.

He recognized a pattern of his sibling's fear of death, for sitting in the back row in a church at a funeral was their strength. How strange his siblings were, but he had to respect their challenges in life. Eventually, every-one will lie in a wooden coffin. After Dingus Sweeney's funeral, Rush and Larlue had a repast at their house. Caesar was never too fond in eating and seeing the older people drink liquor after a funeral. As mourners gathered at the house, the young children would take his death the hardest. Sarah the third youngest sibling would hate her father for dying.

CHAPTER 20
SELF-MASTERY

A few months after the death of the father, Caesar had taken ill again. Lying down in bed with a fever and weak, Caesar listened to his mother and Becky disputing his health.

"Caesar's not dying!" Lucy refused to accept Becky's diagnosis.

"You can't take care of him. He's dying...You lost a lot of time watching daddy die. Now Caesar. Accept it, mother. Please," Becky said, tried pleading to her mother.

"No Becky," Lucy said, whipping her face clean with her hands.

"What good would he do dying here…I had hoped," Becky suggested.

"This is a bad idea. The boy is jus' sick. He'll gets well soon. Becky, give yore brother time." This was the mother's sixth sense of her son, and she knew her son's triumphs too well. Becky left the house for several hours while Lucy comforted...She returned hours later.

"Where have you been, Becky?" Lucy asked. There was no response from Becky.

"I will be working at a politician's house this Wednesday. The politician requested I bake his favorite lasagna dish. Make sure the children are feed. I won't be home early," said Lucy. Rebellious towards her mother's request, Becky gave Matthew a handwritten letter and directed him to take the letter to the telephone exchange station.

Wednesday morning, Lucy prepared herself for work...Lucy kissed her children goodbye and headed out the door for work. The children played outside the front yard enjoying a day of spring games.

A surprising cool breeze of air filtered the children's laughter and screams coming from their playful games.

There was a knock on the front door. Caesar opened his eyes, and there stood a black man in a white uniform over his bed with a pinched look on his face. The man questioned Becky about Caesar's identity, height, weight, age, hair color, and the color of his eyes, their mother's maiden name, and their father's first and last name.

"Are you sure? You want us to take him?" the man asked.

"Take him away," Becky said with an evil grin.

Caesar in a weak voice contested his condition, for he was recovering from bronchitis. The man was unsure how to take him, for he gently positioned his arms under Caesar's body, a surprise electric shock zapped the man's arms. The lamp light flickered. The man released Caesar, giving him a couple of seconds to question his self-mastery. The man picked Caesar fragile body up again. His body became heavy, Caesar cried in resistance. "No, don't take me away."

"Why?"

"Why are you doin' this to me?"

"Becky, no!"

"No Becky, don't let them take me, Becky."

"Momma!"

"Momma!" Caesar screamed again.

"O' Lord, what have you done?" Caesar asked Becky.

"What have you done Becky?" Caesar cried out to Becky.

Becky twisted, hollow smile on her face, brazenly, denying her brother's existence. She stood next to her father's desk with no conscious; there was evil, deception for her brother. His left hand clinched onto the cotton sheet. He spontaneously grabbed the brown pillowcase filled with the memorabilia that his father gave him. Unable to fight the man off, his body had become weak and fragile. The man carried him away and placed him in the back seat of the car. Caesar was driven to Charity Hospital where he was taken to the fifth floor, where he was transferred to a hospital bed. A nurse placed a white bed sheet over his body except for his face.

CHAPTER 21

HE BUILDS CASTLES

In a cold, dark room was little light beaming through the windows. Death was around Caesar from the neighboring dying. The cold of the room was hollow while bodies of the dying lay helpless in their beds.

His body was cold, but his heart was strong, and his mind was solid to survive.

Caesar thought it would be safe for him to think about his mother. She had always been a good mother and yet, good did not describe her. A good mother has a touch of greatness that would be more descriptive of Lucy. She must have been a striking child, growing on her father's farm, learning to accept responsibilities at an early age—

It was a bright shiny Tuesday morning, the blue sky showed a perfect reflection of indulgence. Caesar sat at the family table eating his oatmeal and observing his mother writing out her grocery list before walking into town.

After he had finished breakfast, he bathed before leaving for town. He waited for his mother outside sitting on the steps while Caesar's younger siblings played in the yard, running, jumping, and being a little mouthy with Naomi's children.

Standing next to the steps was Old Ned, a special animal that was given to the Sweeney after the death of Aunt Phoebe.

Waiting for his mother to come outside, Caesar pictured her erect carriage, her shoulders always back with her long silky, black hair falling in gentle waves to her waist. She never ironed her hair. She had high cheekbones, a distinct mulatto mouth that attested to her heritage, and a pair of warm dark eyes that spoke strength and faith. She was quiet, calm, and a confident woman.

She would always sing in her low, throaty voice. One would have to listen closely; to catch the words she sang softly. She had a strong, gentle touch and she never spanked her children. The spankings were left the father. The children were always in danger from one of her backhands, when she had reached the end of her patience, brought on by some form of mischief, a thing that the boys were constantly into at home...

She always kept iodine, calamine lotions, Vaseline, and her own remedies handy, for the many cuts, bruises, bites and stings that the children would run to her for. When applied, the necessary remedy was with such tenderness and care, it would be quite impossible to continue crying. Sometimes her doctoring was accompanied by the bright twinkle in her eyes, and her gentle smile. One would just have to believe that God was in Heaven and had sent one of his angels to set the world right again.

The weather began to warm up. Caesar's mother had no choice, but to roll her hair up into a large bun that sat at the nape of her neck. She wore a lightly starched print dress with the scent of talcum powder, as she perspired, delicately scenting the air around her, but that only added a glow to her copper colored skin. Caesar was happy that he was finally going shopping with his mother and getting away from Naomi and her children 'the wrecking crew'.

Walking down a dry road, Caesar and Lucy passed large white houses, eventually, finding themselves walking through a small town. Walking past business signs that said, "Whites Only," and posters nailed on theater doors with women's and men's faces painted with black makeup. This was his mother's regular route to Jena. They both approached another small town that had a school with a playground, houses with backyard tennis courts, swimming pools, a gazebo and a park picnic area. Next, they came upon a large covered shed with two rows of benches, a bus station, the telephone exchange station, the barbershop that read, "Whites Only." Caesar and his mother finally arrived at the post office, waiting for the mail carrier to be distributed in the mailboxes.

The Sweeney family mailbox number was thirty-seven. She stood chatting with her black friends and white friends, for this was common ground, where everyone felt free to speak to one another. She gathered the mail and placed it in her purse that included a "Sears" catalog. They both walk to the Commissary, which was a huge white-painted building opposite of the Post Office.

When entering the Commissary, Caesar saw several ascending steps that led to a wide veranda that ran two-thirds the length of the building. Shoppers had to pass through a set of thick glass doors, finally finding themselves in a high ceiling warehouse.

Next, passing the stationery, the hardware section that displayed handsaws and hammers in glass showcases.

Finally, arriving at the grocery department, Lucy bought milk, eggs, and meats.

After paying for her selection of groceries, the clerk bagged the paid items. She gave the small grocery bags to Caesar. He lagged far behind his mother while she shopped in the women's department.

After walking the entire store, they both returned to the grocery section; Lucy remembering that she needed to buy some vanilla abstract. The store manager gave her permission to walk through the grocery department with her bags to pick up and purchase the vanilla extract. She decided to make a few more purchases, and before returning for home, they walked over to the candy section.

He thought she would never see it. There she bought a small bag of Fireballs and Jawbreakers that she had handpicked. "Pick a piece of candy," she said with a bright smile on her face. Reaching down in the brown paper bag, Caesar pulled out a Jawbreaker.

She rewarded him with a piece of candy right there on the spot, after which they made their exit out of the Commissary, heading back home. For their return home, she took him through a different path, one that led around business offices.

Walking across a set of railroad tracks, Caesar was told where Mr. Sutton, the director of the hard mill lived.

Next, they followed the boardwalk to its end. At that point, Caesar and his mother found themselves in the colored section of town. They passed small houses and a house where the elementary and junior high school teacher Mrs. Brown lived. They continued their walk, passing a relative's house, the Neals, the schoolhouse, and the Morning Star Baptist Church.

At their arrival, back home was none too soon for Caesar. He was tired to the point of exhaustion, for it had been an extremely hot, long day, and the Jawbreaker had dissolved in his mouth...The memories traveling with his mother, he would remember in 1932—

CHAPTER 22
THE COUNSEL

In the darkness, Caesar heard and saw death around him. The cracking sounds of the walls, the spirits from the dead made their presence known, and the creaking steps paced the ceramic floor.

Their spirits walked with lights of souls,
Far from exhibition lights,
Their spirits passed one-by-one.

Figures of spirits, their souls,
The drum of exhibition.
What can one see?

The spirit completed with brightness,
Given, one spirit, one soul, special gifts,
God's given to see the exhibition.

"And his name, through faith in his name, hath made this man strong, whom ye see and know; yea, the faith which is by him hath given him this perfect soundness in the presence of you all."

— Acts 3:16.

I refuse to die.
I refuse to be silent.
I refuse to lay down my armor.
He always win's our strength.
My strength is the Lord's triumph.

"The triumph that has been hardened upon me, I will survive the cruelty of the world. I accept the conditions in which I am to live. If it had not been for you Lord I would not had been able to see my elders, for my ancestors have strengthened my life. God is powerful. God is great. God is worthy. The master that I serve, to God to be…I am scared of God and what He can do. My Lord and Savior Christ Jesus is the mountain of my pillar. Amen."

A few hours later, a nurse walked into the room. She noticed Caesar wide-awake.

The nurse walked over to him and with a stethoscope, she listened to his heart beating strong and fast.

"Go call the doctor," the nurse ordered the aide nurse.

The doctor questioned the mystery of Caesar's health. He was alive and alert. The doctor readmitted him to the second floor at Charity Hospital in the early morning of June 1938. Caesar would have to undergo several operations in the upcoming months.

His trouble was an old chronic emphysema, which had been bothering him for three years. The chest, lungs, and ribs were explored by a series of x-rays. The x-rays showed a thick fog covering part of the chest cavity, on the left side. The results also concluded that there was an infection in his left lung. In addition, the infection had spread to rib number seven up to number one. The infection was the result of an open wound from a previous operation…was the cause of the exceeded infection…his left lung and ribs.

The first four operations were from previous admissions to Charity Hospital where there had been buildup in the left lung…chronic emphysema since his last discharge from the hospital.

"A thoracoplasty will have to be performed. Floating ribs number eleven and twelve will have to be removed," the chief surgeon said.

"The draining sinus had caused an infection in the left lung. The drainage extended some six to seven inches toward the mid portion of the left lung. Let's explore the sinus," the chief surgeon said. This was an attempt to clear-up a sinus infection successfully.

Operation procedures number twenty: "How are you feeling Caesar?" the collogue surgeon asked.

"I'm okay," Caesar responded.

"Are you ready?" the chief surgeon asked his colleagues assisting him in a series of operations.

"Place him under anesthesia cyclopropane," the chief surgeon ordered the anesthesia nurse.

The chief surgeon and his collogue reopened the left sinus exploring it in detail. The doctors closed the sinus with stitches, and the body was positioned right lateral recumbent.

One nurse carefully cleaned the left hemithorax with ether next to his rib cage. The injured area was painted with mercuric chloride and sterile drapes were placed above the previous thoracoplasty scars. A third small portion of the anterior serratus and posterior latissimus dorsi side was removed.

"To a fair degree, the body heat or the homeostasis is stabilized," the chief surgeon continued, "the patient has been suffering from emphysema. We will have to remove the remaining ribs, false ribs number eight, nine, and ten, including the removal of his left lung."

"What about his heart?" the collogue doctor asked.

"We'll have to reposition the heart, making a passageway for the left heart valve to pass through the right lung," the chief surgeon said. "Isn't that a risk...doctor?" the collogued doctor questioned. His dark-blue eyes scanned the patient's body.

The procedure white mask covered half his face with preparation. And yet he adjusted his bifocals to continue assisting the chief doctor with the operation...

"Let's keep the patient under observation," the chief surgeon responded with confidence in the completion of the surgery.

"Place a Vaseline pack and cover the staples with a pressure dressing..." the collogue doctor ordered the nurse.

During Caesars stay at Charity Hospital, the doctors performed further tests to evaluate his condition. He had the opportunity to explore medicine, for doctors let him draw his own blood. The nurse technician showed him how to insert the needle into his vein to draw his blood with a needle attached to a vial...

The doctors examined the blood specimen to determine the seriousness of his condition. The doctors were kindly enough to let Caesar explore the blood cells through a microscope.

The doctor explained to him the significance of the red and white blood cells. He took an interest in reading books on medicine while residing at Charity Hospital—

Because of his condition he was told he would have a few months to live, which was discouraging news. For there was nothing else the doctors could do for him. Caesar would have to use what time he had left wisely.

He breathes the words.

"I should have taken my last breath of life many years ago. It would have been best if I had just died. My words of faith to victory are useless and fruitless. I have only one lung and half a rib cage. My words of faith for worshiping You is untrustworthy. I wasted my words to save my life, and prospering your words. I have failed God."

The quiet garden that was always filled with colorful roses nourishes the earth's soul. The roses danced with the evening stars, and away in the evening skies a lone bright light made a pathway over an old bridge that stood through the night. The thick foggy clouds shelter and floats across his bedroom window.

He is *unawake.*

CHAPTER 23

THE SERVANT

A blind man stood at the doorway to Caesar's room. He was an elderly man holding some books in his hand. Made of clay and essence, God's children, the blind must comfort and counsel.

He was dressed in a white pullover shirt, with black pants and leather shoes. It became a daily habit for the blind man to stop at the doorway to Caesar's bedroom. However, it would be to say that the blind man would give him a friendly wave.

The blind man sitting at the edge of the bed awoken Caesar from his restless dream. A bright of sunlight beamed inside the window illuminating the freestanding lamp that stood next to his bed.

The blind man placed some books on the cabinet for Caesar to read. "I have no use for them. These books should keep you occupied. According to the order of books, and the book Fruits of Righteousness, a vessel is always filled with knowledge that our tribulation makes us more enduring," the blind man named Paul said.

Annoyed by the blind man, Caesar shrugged his shoulder, "Thank you," Caesar said.

Paul felt the texture of the blanket that covered Caesar's body, "How's your family?"

"I haven't spoken with them for a while. I don't think they know I'm here at Charity Hospital," Caesar responded with emptiness.

"This is yours," Paul said. He hands Caesar a two and a half long natural shaved wood. The wood was perfectly glossed with shellac that shined with beauty and perfection.

Wrapped around each end of the lumber was silver and gold string.

"Do not stumble into his trickery. He wants us to falsify God's Word. He loves pleasuring himself with our troubles and miseries. Never displace your sword. We use our sword for victories and tribulations. Man is fearful only by his own iniquity. Man can learn something about himself when words are repeated to him again. We soon remember our urn that God has given us," Paul expressed with passion to the highest.

"You was baptized in the river, son. Ephesians says it best. Our faith in Christ Jesus," Paul reminded

Caesar. "Blessed be the God and Father of our Lord Je'sus Christ, who hath blessed us with all spiritual blessings in heavenly places in Christ— In whom also we have obtained an inheritance, being predestined according to the purpose of him who worketh all things after the counsel of his own will—In whom ye also trusted, after that ye heard the word of truth, the gospel of your salvation: in whom also, after that ye believed, ye were sealed with that holy Spirit of promise. The eyes of your understanding being enlightened; that ye may know what is the hope of his calling, and what the riches of the glory of his inheritance in the saints. And what is the exceeding greatness of his power to us-ward who believe, according to the working of his mighty power."

—Ephesians 1:3, 11, 13, 18, 19.

"Never separate your love for God which is in Jesus Christ. God loves his children too much. And you should be proud of your victories that are in Christ," Paul said, slowly turning the pages in the Bible.

CHAPTER 24
A VISITOR NAME PAUL

*"And a man shall be as a hiding place from
the wind, and a covert from the tempest: as
rivers of water in a dry place; as the shadow of
a great rock in a weary land."*

—*Isaiah 32:2*

Paul said to Caesar heed an earful: Married at hand
did good deeds for his quarters. After his passing,
members of the quarters began to judge his widowed
and off springs.

A blind woman and her offsprings were under duress
by the fellow citizens. The mother and her seeds, asked
the older vein seed for help. They were under distress by

the quartering that they were sheltered under. The blind mother and her children plead to the vein seed for help.

"I can't help you," the vein seed said. The willing desire to possess illuminating stories is the obsession of hungry wolves. An offer that one cannot refuse by the poison of his voice, the iniquity desire that he has come to anoint his prey is first by denial and second it is the reality of its own right.

The blind mother again, plead to her vein seed for help. "There's nothing that I can do about it," the vein seed said, unemotionally. The blind woman and her two offspring concluded that they must speak to a salesman for a new abode.

The blind mother and her seeds told their vein seed that they were seeking a new abode. Spoken with anger to her blind mother and siblings, the vein seed tells her partner at hand and his spoilers that her mother and siblings is seeking for a new post. They all spoke, telling the salesman a whimpering story about the blind mother and her two seeds. The salesman began to play his fiddle. He found the three blinds a new abode; however, the blind mother and her two blind seeds discovered that the abode was miserable, stressful, and menacing.

The blind woman and her two blind seeds return to the same salesperson asking for another abode that does not have pain and suffering.

The salesman and the blinds create a special friendship, while they both search for another abode. The salesman builds his cave with motivation.

He stalls, holding out, pleasuring himself, knowing that the blind woman needs an abode, "It will put you in the lion's den, until he decides to turn you loose," Paul warned Caesar.

After the salesman satisfies himself, collecting all the silver and gold that he could from the blind mother and her blind children, the salesman releases them, finding the family a different abode. The salesman had left the blind mother and her blind children good impressions of his hard work and service.

"You have gone through a lot of trouble to get me this abode. Here's some fresh water for you," the blind woman said. The salesman takes the water. He asks the three blinds for a favor. He was in need of some soil to fill his den. The salesman went out of his way to demonstrate to the blinds that the soil was required for his den.

"I won't take advantage of you," the salesman said. The three blinds do not hesitate, giving the salesman some soil.

"You're an angel," the salesman said.

Meanwhile, the salesman is dancing. He is indulging in his getting the fresh water and the soil.

A few months passed; the salesman did not return the soil to the blind woman and her children. The blind mother called the salesman inquiring about her soil. The salesman's response, "I don't have it. I'm still waiting for the other abodes to sell. Hold on, I'll give you back your soil." The salesman goes to his passage tunnel spreading the word to his associates, that he had accomplished his goal with the blind man, exciting himself. The blind woman and her children discover that the salesman had sold them a pillar that had the same results from the last abode.

> The salesman calls the blinds, asking for some more soil. The blinds said, "...Praise be to the God of Shadrach, Meshach and Abednego, who has sent his angel and rescued his servants! They trusted in him and defied the king's command and were willing to give their lives rather than serve or worship any god except their own God."
>
> —Daniel 3:28.

For the salesman had gone down in defeat and returned to his cave of darkness. He had lost the battle of vanity.

However, the salesman worked hard with his associates to confuse the blind.

The blind mother and her children do not budge. They are enemies with his bordering associates of the salesman. The blind mother and her children liberate their victory, for they rebuild their relationship with their God.

"Yes nothing. Nothing can separate the love of God, which is in Jesus Christ. You are not in condemnation. Jesus was led by the Spirit into the desert, where he was tempted by the devil. Jesus fasted for forty days and forty nights, and with hunger and thirst Jesus refused to listen and be tempted by evil, for the Lord had the word's truth in his heart. God is too proud of his victories to let you go. But, the salesman deceived God's children, telling God's children they can't believe in the Bible. Refuse the devil. Don't believe in his trickery. Ask yourself who is the seed of evil? You want the blood to pass through you. The blood of Jesus gives us the strength to live, to survive, and to see. The blood makes it complete and cleanse us. The blood. The blood. The blood. The blood. The blood covers us all. What has God done for you? God will plant your feet on solid ground when your trials and tribulations are tested, while everyone around you has fallen down," Paul reminded Caesar.

"The power of God, you are covered by the lamb. The beating drum knows the truth of everything we are and what we exercise to be *spirit, fate, growth*. And that is *life*. Your triumph is the Lord's victory. The blood is Jesus. The blood covers you, by the blood of the lamb. And you should be proud of your victories that are in Christ." Paul continued, "Thank you Lord, for your comfort in my life. I draw near to you and seek your comfort today. Thank you for your mercies and that they are known every morning when I awaken. He is the Holy Ghost. I say to the Lord's children, paying the ultimate price to live in courage, reality, strength, bravery, and survive challenges, is the response to God who is in the son of Christ. Remember that you are a winner, if you believe, you are. Confidence in yourself will make you a winner," Paul gave Caesar his blessing.

When Paul left Caesar's bedroom, Caesar felt anointed by Paul's words of courage to live, rejoice and be glad. He asked the Lord for redemption and forgiveness. Paul did not return after that day, but left Caesar's bedside with enlightened words of wisdom and courage.

Caesar rehabilitated himself to God the father of Christ Jesus the Lord; he again consults with God.

Caesar gazed outside the window. A thick fog formed into the shape of a man dressed in a long white and gray gown. His hair and beard flowed loosely and gracefully down his gown. He was a tall man with a wide nose. His face was bony square with a projecting jaw. His figure body walked across the pathway over an old bridge that stood outside his bedroom window:

Again, I shall not lay my armor down.
He, I worship each day and praise.
You are a beating drum without limits.
God is my victory.
I know who I am, Caesar Sweeney.

"I worship our mighty King, my Christ Jesus our Lord. He, I worship each day and praise. I can make it. I will survive. I will win. I must live, my vessels are designed of clay of God…" Caesar thought of the memories of his mother and father's second flower garden that his mother loved the most. There she grew her favorite flowers, red, yellow, and pink roses. She was not happy unless she grew honeysuckles each year. The blossom of the honeysuckles would perfume the air, especially at nighttime.

CHAPTER 25
THE HAPPIEST TIMES

After Caesar's mother would finish her housework, she would sit with her husband outside watching the sky light up with stars, glittering in the dark sky, large as buckets. Caesar and his siblings would sit on the edge of the porch with their feet dangling, searching the sky for falling stars, pointing and exclaiming loudly each time one speckled across the line of sight.

At times, the children would play such a game to see who could spot a falling star first, and then fall asleep on the grass to be carried to bed by on their mother and father's shoulders…

Even when the parents could not afford toys for the children, the happiest times were always Christmas. However, the cold winter would not stop Caesar's father from finding a Christmas for the family in the deep forest.

"Look Daddy!" Caesar said excited, pointing to a large Christmas tree that stood to be seven feet tall. The beauty of a large Scotch pine tree, its stiff branches, and dark-green needles was attractive.

"Move back, Caesar. Move back, Samuel," Dingus said. He used his favorite saw to cut down the Christmas tree. Dingus sawed back and forth, keeping a straight line.

The scotch tree fell making a tiny quivering sound. Before taking the tree home, Dingus examined the tree, making sure the tree was free from insects and spiders. With all of his strength, Dingus pulled the tree to the wagon. He lifted up the tree, placing it into the wagon.

"Giddy up Old Ned," shouted Dingus. The ride back home was filled with the fresh aroma of scented pine that filtered the air. There had always been something special about the scotch tree, the long-lasting freshness that lasted throughout the season, and the survival rate of such a Christmas tree was first class. Most importantly, the Scotch pine was always easy to replant for the next coming Christmas. Although the Scotch pine was not white, there was always the dream of having a white Christmas. However, the fresh green tree that always stood bare, no gifts and ornaments, during Christmas time was a reminder that Christmas was a time to celebrate the birth of Jesus and to share the authentic memories.

The elders and the children would sit around the bare Christmas tree with songs to celebrate the birth of Jesus, and they would sing:

Jesus, Our Christ and savior born.
A northern star shines bright,
We rejoice, Jesus.

Mother of Jesus,
Joy of gifts,
With gifts and prayers,
We rejoice, Jesus.

He is blessed with gold and frankincense,
Jesus, Our Christ and savior born.

We rejoice our King from Heaven.

Our gifts to you our lord,
Jesus, Our Christ and savior is born.
Jesus, Our Christ and savior is born.

Caesar's family was thankful for what they had, and that was each other. Christmas was a time to think about family, health, and security—

In springtime, Lucy was always eager to get an early start in her garden. On some occasions, Dingus would hire Mr. Bryant, who had a team of farmers and a mule to plow the garden.

What fun the kids would have seeing their father wrestle with a balky old mule and hear him curse at the animal.

Lucy would chase the children away from hearing such language from Dingus, but not for long. The children would sneak quickly back, listening to such vulgar language from their father. After plowing the soil, the younger children would play in the newly turned, warm earth of dirt.

Lucy loved to work outdoors in her garden. She would grow such beautiful vegetables, okra, string beans, tomatoes, corn, peppers, squash, and other sorts of vegetables. The produce that came from her garden would put the vegetables at the Commissary to shame.

The kids would water their mother's garden, keeping it fresh and contained. The children learned to garden by choice, and it was survival that they would need one day. The children would keep their mother's garden free from dead weeds by pulling up the wild flowers that grew tall from the fresh dirt.

Lucy was born with a green thumb. She could raise almost anything that would grow with water, sunshine, and tender loving care. Caesar could not argue that his mother had the sheer guts and courage to shoulder the full responsibilities for such a large family.

Yes, she had that and more.

CHAPTER 26
LETTERS TO MY DEAREST MOTHER

November 5, 1938

Dear mom,

I'm here at Charity Hospital. The doctors saw that I was still alive and breathing...

I'm here on the third floor recovering from several operations.

I hope everything is well with you and the kids. I hope to hear from you and my brothers and sisters soon. I had lost a lot of blood. I had a blood transfusion, not too long after being admitted. I'm now a type O negative.

Love,
Caesar

November 12, 1940

Dear mom,

Haven't heard from you and my siblings, I hope everything is okay. I want to see you and the kids. Today, the doctors had to remove two more ribs on the left side of my body. The nurses here at Charity Hospital are treating me well. I have been reading books to keep myself occupied.

The hospital has a library of books that I took interest in–Ernest Hemingway, James Baldwin, John Beecroft, and Mika Waltari are four of my favorite authors, and I love listening to Mahalia Jackson.

I miss you dearly and I hope to see you soon.

Love, your son Caesar

February 27, 1944

Dear mom,

Years have passed, I haven't heard from you or the kids. I never received any returned letters from you or my brothers and sisters. I know I'm writing to the correct home address. This week the doctors let me draw my own blood and examine the blood cells through the microscope. I'm going to need another blood transfusion.

My kidneys are not functioning normally and the doctors will explore this condition further. I'm beginning to learn how to type. The doctors gave me a journal to write important medical information.

This information has helped me understand the circumstances behind my operations.

Love you and my brothers and sisters.

Your son,

Caesar

June 15, 1946

Dear mom and family,

I'm recovering from what hopefully will be my last operation. I had my left lung removed. The doctors had to push my heart over to the right side, next to my right lung. Right now, it's hard for me to breathe with one lung, but I'm taking breathing treatments to help me breathe better. Mother, I miss you and I think about dad every day. I had a dream about dad the other night. He's smiling in Heaven. I know he is watching over you and the kids. The future of becoming is not an easy thing to accept, but I will have to accept the terms and conditions of the forthcomings.

I will continue to write to you, knowing that I still love you and I will always be your son. If you get this letter, tell Aunt Estella and Uncle Richard I will be coming to visit them when I am released from Charity Hospital.

Love always,
Caesar Douglas Sweeney

CHAPTER 27
HOW FAR CAN I GO?

September 1946, at the age of twenty-three Caesar was discharged from the hospital. He paid for a one-way coach ticket to St. Louis, Missouri. The female nurse from the hospital helped him board the Mississippi train, seating him in the white section...and with good-byes, she handed him an envelope, postmarked from Los Angeles...

He gripped the letter tightly hoping that it was from his mother. The Jim Crow laws that made it unlawful for blacks and whites to integrate into public transportation that included buses, trains, public schools, colleges, restaurants, bathrooms, and clubs. However, Caesar thought he would take his chances. A white man noticed him on the train. A man waved for the conductor.

"What is that nigger doing on this train? He needs to be with those other people. You know where they belong." The conductor was sympathetic with the mistreatment of blacks, but he could not show his protest against the Jim Crow laws.

"There's no justice in America. Next thing you know, they'll be riding free on our trains," the angry white male gestured.

"You ain't gonna cause trouble on this train?" the conductor asked.

"No sir," Caesar replied.

He reminded the conductor of the money that he had paid to sit coach.

"I'll see how far I can go. I paid my fare." The conductor walked back to the front of the entrance to the train. The whistle blew loudly...the last passengers boarded the train.

"One hour, and fifty-five minutes to the next stop," the conductor loudly announced.

Caesar stared out the window while the white people took quick looks at a black man on the train. Caesar was excluded from being served complimentary packages of peanuts, coffee, and wine that were given to the passengers.

An hour into the ride the train began climbing in the deep mountains. The wheels turned slowly.

The wheels moved in sequence...the train made a distinct sound.

Listening closely, he heard the sound of men pounding and connecting the jointing tracks to the joint bars between the two-bullhead rails. The loud hammering sound of the wheels on the train generated a herd of stampeding Buffaloes.

Caesar taking his mind off of the pounding and hammering sound from the wheels, decided to read the letter given to him earlier.

August 28, 1946

Dear Caesar,

I haven't had the chance to write to you. I've been busy working and cleaning houses. In 1942, Henry was drafted into the Army. He's stationed in Italy. Your brother Samuel was drafted into the Navy. He was drafted three months after Henry.

In 1943, Matthew signed up for the Army, he's now back home. He's learning to be an electrician. Your baby brother Adam is growing fast. He's a spoiled child. Becky buys him things he doesn't need. Your Uncle Rush passed away last year. He's buried not too far from Charles II and your father Dingus. Naomi's children are practically grown.

The oldest child got himself in trouble with the law. He's spending time in prison.

Becky has a son name Frank. Becky and Frank are living with your younger siblings and me.

Naomi decided to move to California with her kids; she found a job working for a company near Los Angeles. She said that it was best for us to move to California…I sold what all I had at the house and we all moved to California in April 1945.

By the way, Becky applied and submitted your death certificate in Clarks. I don't know how or what you will need to cancel the death certificate. Aunt Estella and your Uncle Richard know you're on your way to Missouri.

Love,
Your mother, Lucy

"—How did you get on this train boy?" a heavyset white man asked. The thoughts and memories of Caesar's family became a quick distraction coming from a white passenger…

"On my way to Missouri. Sir," Caesar replied. The man returned to his seat, with hateful words. Caesar prayed with faith that he would reach his destination, even if it took him some time to get to Missouri.

Caesar stared out the window and he noticed the black passengers were entering the back of the train. "I'm gonna kill that nigger," a white man uttered, sitting in a seat in front of him.

Caesar knew the threat was for him.

"I believe you dropped this sir," a black man said, in his mid-twenties, dressed in a conductor uniform. He passed Caesar a crumple piece of paper from behind.

"I wish I had your courage. Get off at the next stop. I'll be at the front of the train. If they ask, do you know me? You say, no sir."

Caesar tucked the note in his white pocket shirt. While waiting for the next stop, he noticed something was tapping on his head. He reached for his head and noticed it was saliva. There was a white man lying down on an overhead compartment of the train. The man was spitting on Caesar's head.

"Wha cha' gonna to do, nigger?" Caesar knew that he would be in trouble if he answered back.

'Clickety-clack,' there was the screech of wheels braking.

The screech of the wheels braking, accompanied the strong bump of cargo cars attached to the train that speedily stopped. The man rolled out from the overhead compartment, landing on the floor staring at Caesar's shoes and his long legs.

"What are you doing down there, boy?" The conductor yelled at the white man. After the man got up from his embarrassing fall, Caesar followed behind the white passengers exiting off the train.

"Go to the middle outhouse. Can you make it, champ?" the black man said.

"Yes," Caesar replied, briefly.

"Do you know this boy?" the conductor said, snappily.

"No sir," the black man said.

"By the way, the company doesn't need you anymore," the conductor added. The man thought this was a good opportunity for him to work full-time at his father's nightclub.

"Go get your paycheck," the conductor said heatedly.

"Yassuh. Yassuh. I'se on my way."

The man went to pick up his last pay, carrying a military backpack. Caesar hid in the outhouse waiting for the man to come. The black man handed Caesar a brown shirt, and a pair of pants to change into.

"Man, you got some big feet. How tall are you?" he said, measuring Caesar's height.

"Here put these shoes on. You got to be at least six feet tall."

"I guess so," Caesar said. The man could not help but notice the left side of his back. There were patches of cotton bandages covering his recent operations.

"What happened to your back?" Caesar briefly explained his injury to the man.

The two men walked behind the shed that led to a hilly trail. Caesar used all of his strength to make it to his destination.

"Here, drink some of this cold water," the man said, handing him a canteen…They both continued to walk down the road, when they saw a car driving in the opposite direction.

The man pulled Caesar by the shirt.

"Hurry up!" Caesar ran fast as his long legs could, holding his chest, and gasping for air. The two men found themselves in an outhouse that stunk from the perfume of a skunk. The car stopped at the outhouse, and three men got out of the car. The men were dressed in white robes and pointed hoods covering their faces. One of the men pounded on the outhouse door that was locked from the inside.

"Hurry up in there!"

"Hurry up! I gots to pee badly." Caesar and the man's bones were solid as a rock. Not one single joint popped for readjusting.

The smell of a skunk did its job, buying time for the two men. They saw the men dressed in Klan's uniform from a peephole that was carved out from the outhouse.

"Hurry up! We haven't got all-day. Smell…stinky hell around here," the Klan's man gestured.

After the men had finished relieving themselves in front of the outhouse, they walk back to the car and drove off.

Darkness swiftly approached…the man and Caesar continued their walk down a dusty road.

"I'm Caesar Sweeney. I didn't get your name?"

"Tom Carter," he responded.

Finally, reaching Tom's parents' house, Caesar knew he was now safe.

CHAPTER 28
LANGUAGE AND DETERMINATION

Tom removed a string around his neck that had a key attached to it. He unlocked the front door with the house key, where his parents sat comfortably on their sofa.

His brother Jubilee was sitting on the floor reading a book, his father reading a newspaper and his mother knitting.

"New band member?" Mr. Carter said, giving Caesar a bright smile.

"No dad, his name is Caesar Sweeney. He was sitting in the coach part of the train," Tom responded.

"What in the world where you doing riding in the white section of the train? Did that myself…made it all the way from Georgia to Mississippi," Mr. Carter said, and then laughed at his own words.

"We have to hide him," Tom said.

"Joanne, honey make a bed for Caesar," Mr. Carter said, smiling. Mrs. Carter stopped knitting to lay down a bed for him to sleep on.

"Thank you kindly," Caesar said. He explained to Mr. Carter that he did not have much money to give them, but he would work for them to pay his debt back to the family.

Coming back from turning a bed down, Mrs. Carter sat next to her husband on the coach—as Caesar continued to tell his story. Mr. and Mrs. Carter reassured Caesar that he had nothing to worry about with them.

"Are you hungry Caesar?" Mrs. Carter asked.

He responded in a weak voice, "Yes ma'am." However, before they all ate dinner, she guided Caesar to the bedroom, she cleaned his wound with a gauze and cleaning solution.

Tom walked into the bedroom, handing Caesar a clean pair of men's pajamas to wear.

After cleaning his wounds, they both walked to the dining room. An extra chair was placed at the dinner table for Caesar to sit.

Mrs. Carter served her old-fashioned beef stew and her favorite peach cobbler for dessert. Caesar was already stuffed, but could not turn down the fresh smell of a homemade peach cobbler.

"You and my mother make the best peach cobbler!" Caesar said. That praise put a big smile on her face. After eating dessert, Mr. Carter and his two sons decided to play dominoes, checkers, and discuss town and neighbor gossip in the family room.

Caesar helped Mrs. Carter clear the dining table. She suggested that he join the family in the living room, but he insisted on helping her, reiterating his debt to the family. Mrs. Carter reasoned with him to help her clear the dinner table…

"Sit here," Tom said, ushering Caesar to an empty chair next to his. Tom was not good at the game, dominoes, but Caesar caught on to the game quickly. He could not help Tom's bad score, for it was too late. Turning in for the night, they all went to their prospective rooms, all wishing Caesar a good night's sleep. The linen on the bed was the fresh smell that allowed him to adjust his body comfortably in the bed. While staring outside the window, the sharp reflection of his glasses beamed off the clear window. Caesar removed his glasses and began to think about the weight of the world. Receiving charity is an appreciation of heart, and paying it forward is automatic for those who believe in righteousness.

He closed his eyes and slept comfortably through the night—

"Are you asleep, Caesar?" It was Mrs. Carter speaking in a hoarse morning voice.

"No Mrs. Carter. I'm getting up," Caesar answered back, wiping sleep from his eyes.

"Would you like some coffee?" Mrs. Carter asked, yawning than sipping on a cup of fresh coffee.

"Yes, ma'am."

"I'll bring you a cup."

Mrs. Carter knocked on the door, before walking into the bedroom. She brought him a fresh cup of hot coffee, and another cup filled with sugar.

After finishing his cup of coffee, he bathed before appearing to the Carters.

"Tom. You're gonna be late for work," Mr. Carter shouted, in the living room.

"Good morning, Mr. Carter," Caesar said.

Mr. Carter replied with a friendly good morning. Walking in the living room where Mr. Carter sat in his favorite chair.

"I noticed your back garden. Does it need plowing?" Caesar asked.

"Yes, son. I don't want you doing too much. My wife said your scars are not fully healed. We don't want you to die on us. We've already had one death here at the house, my wife's grandmother," Mr. Carter said.

"I promise. I won't do too much, Mr. Carter," Caesar responded.

"Make sure you get some rest, eat, and drink water. We both can turn the dirt together," Mr. Carter suggested.

"And make sure you drink some of my mother's delicious lemonade," Tom added, walking out the bathroom with a towel over his head.

Standing in the doorway to the kitchen was Mrs. Carter, stirring a pan of hot grits, "Aren't you gonna be late for work?" Mrs. Carter asked.

"They let me go. They don't need me anymore," Tom said.

"Can't be the economy," Jubilee said.

"What do you know about the economics?"

"Ah, leave your brother alone," Mr. Carter said.

"I'm just teasing him. You're all right, Jubilee," Tom tapping his brother on the shoulder; he continued, "now I can play my Georgia all day long."

"Caesar, that's his saxophone," Mrs. Carter said, walking into the living room, nibbling on a slice of bacon. Tom was talented with the saxophone. People would come from all over Mississippi to hear him and his band play at his father's nightclub. Three black men and an Irishman had a good reputation for their stylish jazz sounds and their spoken vocals words in rap tone.

"Maybe you can come and see us play Thursday, Caesar?" Tom said.

"I would love to...after I do my chores here at the house," Caesar said.

"Don't kill yourself, champ," Tom said.

Mrs. Carter walked back to the kitchen.

"Breakfast's ready!"

After breakfast, Jubilee headed to school…

Tom always made sure his brother made it to school safely, even if it made him late for work. Caesar and Mr. Carter walked through a hallway that led into the backyard. Opening the door, Caesar could smell the fresh scent of large red tomatoes, cucumbers, thyme, and rosemary. The smell of the vegetables and herbs reminded him of home.

Mr. Carter walked to a shed and picked special gardening tools…to work with.

Mrs. Carter opened the back door that led to the garden, "Put this hat on, Caesar," Mrs. Carter said, handing him a straw hat.

Mrs. Carter headed off to work that early morning. She noticed a brown, two-door car parked near a River Birch-Betula nigra tree not too far from their house. She continued her walk to work with caution.

"Mrs. Carter!" Mr. Bayle, yelled, "need a ride to work?" Not hesitating, Mrs. Carter took the neighbor's offer. Mrs. Carter began the conversation admiring Mrs. Bayles' new garden.

"Mr. Bayle, your wife has such a beautiful garden! How's the children?" Mrs. Carter asked, stirring her neighbor away from bringing up the subject about the mysterious car.

"Oh, they're just great. My oldest son will be attending college soon. Johnny my second son, he'll be…" Mr. Bayle responded. The discussion of his family went on for twenty minutes.

Arriving at the hospital safely where Mrs. Carter and Mr. Bayle worked, "I can't thank you enough for the ride to work today," Mrs. Carter said.

"Not a problem. See you and Mr. Carter Thursday night at the club," Mr. Bayle responded.

They both went about their way to their prospective jobs at the hospital.

Back at the Carter's house: Caesar helped Mr. Carter plow the dead grass from the soil. Mr. Turning the soil in spring was common to keep the soil, fresh and moist.

"Let's stop here. After we finish turning the grass, we can spread fertilizer on the dirt." Mr. Carter and Caesar sat down on the steps staring at their accomplishments, pulling up the dead grass from the dirt.

"Is that your handsaw?" Caesar asked.

"Yes, it is. Why?" Mr. Carter replied, wiping sweat from his forehead with a washrag.

"Can you teach me how to saw wood?" Caesar asked bravely. Mr. Carter was hesitant to teach him, but did not want to turn down a young man's determination to learn. Mr. Carter gave Caesar's question some thought and agreed to teach him.

"But after I finish my work and if you're not tired," Caesar said. With agreement, the two men went back to their plowing.

After the two men finished plowing the dirt and grass, Mr. Carter brought out some wood to be sawed. He handed Caesar a ruler, a pencil, and some numbers to measure. The electric saw was placed on a flat wooden table that Mr. Carter made. He gradually guided Caesar's hands as he began sawing a piece of wood.

Mr. Carter gave Caesar another piece of wood to be sawed—

For the next three days, the two men would repeat their tasks, plowing the dirt and grass, and sawing fresh wood.

On one occasion, Mr. Carter showed Caesar how to build a compost bin.

Caesar was good at concentration. He was disciplined, with no complaints from the Carter family.

CHAPTER 29
ORNITHOLOGY

Thursday night was show night at Larrea's Jazz Café, and Tom was excited for the sold out tickets.

"Coming to the club, Caesar?" Tom asked.

"I'll take a rain check," Caesar said.

"See you all later. Mom are you coming to the club tonight?" Tom asked.

"I decided to stay home tonight," Mrs. Carter responded.

"I think we all are gonna turn in for bed early tonight. We all had a long week," Mr. Carter said—

Mr. and Mrs. Carter sat up in their bed debating on the mysterious car that had been driving through the neighborhood.

"I want the boy to stay, but it may scare him…" Mrs. Carter said.

Neighbors also had noticed the strange car in the neighborhood, and it did not sit nicely with them. It was not the sheriff nor a police car, but a car with suspicious people sitting inside—

Larrea's Jazz Café was packed with listeners. It was 9:10 that night, a large crowd had gathered inside the club to hear their favorite jazz music by inspired musicians. Tom's band brought in the majority of the crowd that night, for they would play Duke Ellington, Dizzy Gillespie, and Charlie "Bird" Parker, "Ornithology."

Tom continued to pump out the notes from his saxophone with every breath of air he had to make the notes flow. A distinctive loud sound of notes told the story of struggle and sacrifice.

Back at the Carters house, there was an unexpected knock at the door. Jubilee ran into his parents' bedroom.

"Sheriff Baker's at the door," he said, panicking.

"Take Caesar to the basement. Quickly!" Jubilee obeyed his father's orders and guided Caesar down to the basement.

"Open up," Sheriff Baker yelled, banging on the door with his fist. Mr. Carter walked to the front door, opening the door with Mrs. Carter standing behind her husband.

"Yes, Sheriff Baker?" Mr. Carter said, rubbing his eyes, and scratching his head.

The sheriff was a tall, white man with a black mustache, and black hair. His haircut was in the shape of a high and tight military haircut. "I was told that you were hiding a criminal here at the house," Sheriff Baker said.

"Criminal? What are you talking about, Sheriff Baker? It's just me, my wife, and our wo sons," Mr. Carter responded quickly.

A white man walked up next to the sheriff. "I saw a nigger…and it wasn't your son that works at the train station," the white man said.

"I don't know what you're talking about. Besides, I can have whomever I want in my house. You don't pay my bills," Mr. Carter responded.

"You better watch it, nigger," the white man said.

"WILL YOU SHUT UP? What are you doing around here?" Sheriff Baker said angrily.

"I'm the one who called you to come to arrest that nigger that was on the train."

"Go back to your car and let me handle this," Sheriff Baker shouted.

"Sheriff Baker, you gonna let these niggers get away with—"

"If you don't go back to that car, I'm gonna arrest you for breathing. Now get." The man stubbornly walked back to his car, looking back at Mr. Carter.

"I need to look around or would you like to take care of this down at the station?"

Mr. Carter calmly opened the door. Sheriff Baker noticed a neatly, furnished living room with no sign of any visitor.

The Carter family was aware of the oppressed and segregated Jim Crow Laws, and did not agree with them.

"I think everyone in the community is aware that a Negro man was lynched by the Klan for riding on the coach part of the train, after he'd paid his fine to the county last week," Mr. Carter said. Mr. Carter was not afraid to stand up for himself and his family.

"You were in the Navy?" Sheriff Baker asked. He saw Mrs. Carter standing behind her husband.

"Is that you Joanne? I didn't recognize you," Sheriff Baker said prickly.

"Yes sheriff," Mrs. Carter responded, her hand tightly grasping her husband's pajama shirt.

"Joanne fixed my wound last week," Sheriff Baker bragging with a wiry smile.

"There was a bank robbery two blocks from the hospital and a few police officers were injured. I patched up Sheriff Baker's gunshot wound," Mrs. Carter clarified to her husband.

"—Joanne's the best nurse in the world." Mr. Carter gave the sheriff a half-smile.

"Oh, that incident," Mr. Carter responded unconcerned with Sheriff Baker's injury.

"I'm sorry to have bothered your family. Goodnight," Sheriff Baker said, walking out the door.

"You both will know what will happen if you're hiding a Negro. Fines doubled after three weeks," Sheriff Baker said.

"I'm not gonna argue with you. But us negroes riding on the train is not a crime. We negroes have rights just like white folks, to ride on the train," Mr. Carter words of protest against the Jim Crow laws. Sheriff Baker paused before responding, "you people have a good night."

Sheriff Baker approached the three white men in the brown car. "Go home, and don't let me see any of you boys around in this neighborhood again. Do I make myself clear?" The car sped off without anyone answering Sheriff Baker. Jubilee went and guided Caesar from the basement up to the living room.

Caesar apologized for his stay and problems that he was causing the family...Mr. and Mrs. Carter refused to accept his guilt.

"Everything will be just fine," Mrs. Carter said. The family welcomed Caesar to stay as long as he liked and not to worry about the Klan and the sheriff.

"I need to get to my Aunt Estella," Caesar said, anxiously. Mr. Carter explained that it would be dangerous for him to leave Mississippi. Caesar agreed with Mr. Carter—

"Is everyone okay? I saw the sheriff leaving," Tom said rushing into the house, dripping in sweat.

"Boy, don't you come busting in this house like that. You 'bout to given us all a heart attack," Mr. Carter said angrily, roughly rubbing his face.

"I'm sorry Dad, but I saw the sheriff leaving the neighborhood," Tom said.

"Well, you missed the party, including the Klan," Mr. Carter responded.

"You all right, Caesar?" Tom asked.

"Yeah, I'm just a little shaken-up, but I'll be, okay," Caesar responded.

Fear is in all men, but courage and spirit is strong and never forgotten. Everyone went to bed except Mr. Carter and Caesar, both shaken-up over the test of racism.

"Tell me the history of the Jim Crow laws?" Caesar asked. Mr. Carter said that it would be separate, but equal laws that created oppression, depression, discrimination, and black suffrage.

The Southern states wanted to control the Northern states that included the railroad and transportation industry. Southern states wanted to count blacks as three-fifth of the population, control labor, and labor wages, transporting good, education, and economic institutions.

The Northern states wanted free labor, economic stability. Northern states began to question the Reconstruction in the South, giving most but not all Northern states reasons for wanting to end slavery. Blacks were no longer chattel slaves without equal rights.

The freedom for blacks would be the beginning of the black suffrage in the Americas. Black would not be liberated in the South, for blacks in the South had to follow harsh laws.

With the Jim Crow laws and conditions, Negroes had to live by these rules or pay the consequences.

Caesar's memories of the walk he had taken with his mother to the Commissary were now clear—

The end of November approached, and it was the last Sunday of the month, with the Carters. He would be heading to his next destination, Tennessee.

Night came, the men waited to make their move to sneak Caesar out of the house, for the moon was stubborn to hide its light from the earth.

"Are you sure your father will let Caesar stay with him?" Tom asked Myles. Jewel Parker and his wife Carol had been residing with Mr. Scott for a while, after losing their house to a hurricane four years ago. Parker was also a bodybuilder whose trainer was Mr. Scott. He continued, "Parker and his wife moved to Memphis, Tennessee last year...He's the one that won the National Body-Building Championship!" Myles reminded Tom.

"—With all this talk about bodybuilding, how long is it going to take you all to drive to Tennessee?" Mr. Carter asked.

"With Myles driving, maybe around two to three hours," Tom replied.

"That's without speeding, Mr. and Mrs. Carter. We'll take good care of Caesar," Myles said. Mr. Carter hoped that Tom and Myles would keep their word...

Mrs. Carter gave Caesar a kiss on his forehead, for she did not want to see Caesar leave.

She walked to the kitchen after her goodbye kiss to Caesar with tears rolling down her face. She could not bear to see him go. Mr. Carter and Jubilee struggled to hold back their tears, both giving their hugs to Caesar.

Tom, Myles and the other two band members waited for Caesar to arrive at the vehicle. The moon hid its face behind the dark clouds. The darkness from the world would not entertain the company of the moon to shine through the sky. Caesar walked out of the house into the world, with no fear and no ignorance of humanity. Tom, Myles, and Caesar would travel to Tennessee while the other two members of the band drove to Arkansas. Myles, Tom, and the other two men agreed to meet in Chicago in two weeks.

The three men drove off traveling through the night. Tom, Myles, and Caesar agreed to take a break before arriving in Tennessee. After an hour's drive, the men pulled into a gas station located a hundred and twenty miles from Tennessee.

After filling the car up with gas, checking the oil and the tires, Myles drove his car into an empty parking space.

The men sat inside the car eating some ham sandwiches and a batch of orange cookies. The buttery taste of the orange cookies, a ham sandwich, and a soda pop made a perfect meal.

"Drive us to Tennessee!" Myles said, handing Tom the car keys.

CHAPTER 30

WATCH YOUR SPEED

The road sign posted read, "One hundred thirty miles." The ride to Tennessee would soon stop as a dark, black-and-white car drifted fast next to the car.

"Thanks a lot Myles. You jinxed me. They must have heard you a mile away," Tom said.

"Just stay calm," Myles responded. Tom pulled the car off the road, turned off the ignition, and placed both of his hands on the steering wheel. All three men sat still until the two officers approached the car. Tom rolled down the window.

One officer stood on the passenger side of the car, while the other officer approached the driver's side. The two police officers shined their flashlights inside the car.

"Where you all headed?" Before Tom could respond to the officer's question, he said, "I need for you all to step out of the car," the police offer said. The three men got out of the car.

"I need to see you all drivers' licenses…" the officer said. Tom handed the officer his driver's license.

"What about you?"

"He doesn't have one officer," Tom responded.

"I'm not talking to you, boy," the officer said.

"I don't have one, sir," Caesar answered the police officer with his glasses beaming in the officer's eyes.

"How old are you, boy? You look too young to drive, anyway," the police officer asked. The other officer pulled out a piece of paper.

"Have you seen this person?" He directed the question to Caesar. He took a good look at a sketch of a black man wanted for robbery in Tennessee.

"No sir," Caesar responded.

"Who's the owner of this vehicle?" the police officer asked.

"I am," Myles responded.

"I suggest you three keep driving and don't stop 'til you get to where you all supposed to be," the officer said.

"Yassuh," all three men answered in chorus. Tom returned to the driver's seat while Caesar climbed in the backseat and Myles sat in the front passenger seat.

"Watch your speed limit, Tom," Myles suggested looking through his side view mirror.

"Yeah, that's not all I better watch!"

"You okay back there, Caesar?" Myles asked.

"Not yet, but I will be," Caesar responded—

Forty-five minutes into the drive, there was a large road sign that read, "Welcome to the State of Tennessee."

Tom continued driving to their destination, where they smelled a mile away, the strong aroma of grits, eggs, bacon, sausage, hot coffee, and fresh homemade biscuits. The men's noses investigated the cooking coming from the house up ahead.

"Smells like my mother's cooking," Tom said, driving down a residential street, investigating where the aroma was coming from.

"You're right on that Tom. Smells like my mother's cooking too," Caesar said, smiled.

"Don't get me wrong, Myles. Your father can cook, but it doesn't smell like his cooking," Tom pondered.

"All right, you guys got me." Myles, Tom, and Caesar saw light in Mr. Scott's house.

The three men entered the house where there was Parker sitting on the couch, sipping on a fresh cup of hot coffee.

"Got company, Pa," Myles yelled walking passed the den to his father's bedroom and continued, "have a seat, men."

Mr. Scott approached from the kitchen door.

"How's it going?" Mr. Scott asked.

"Great, just great," Tom said greeting Mr. Scott with a handshake.

"So, you're Caesar?" Mr. Scott responded.

"Well, Caesar you're welcome at my house anytime." A friendly gesture from Mr. Scott.

A black woman appeared in a beautiful, bright yellow flower dress. All the men stopped to notice her smooth facial features with almond skin and dark-brown eyes.

"I like for you all to meet my wife, Mrs. Thelma Scott," Mr. Scott proudly introduced his wife to the three men.

"Good morning, gentlemen," Mrs. Scott said brightly. The three responded 'good morning in unison.

"Breakfast is ready, men," she softly announced. Mrs. Scott had prepared breakfast for five hungry men who were ready to grub down fried chicken, breakfast sausages, biscuits, scrambled eggs, and a hot pot of coffee.

Sitting at the table, their priority was eating with no table discussions allowed. The sound of the silverware tapping the coffee cup, mixing the sugar into the coffee, and the scraping of the knives and forks on the China plates, was in response to the good cooking of Mrs. Scott.

After breakfast, Myles and Tom had to leave, for they had to meet their other band members in Chicago.

"Take good care of Caesar, Pa," Myles said holding his father to his word.

"I will, don't you two worry about Caesar. He'll be all right with us," Mr. Scott said.

Myles and Tom said their goodbyes to Caesar and Parker. The two men gave Mrs. Scott a goodbye kiss on her fluffy, brown cheeks.

CHAPTER 31
BRANDING A SPEECH

M r. Scott directed Caesar to his bedroom. "This will be your room," Mr. Scott said.

"What can I do around the house to help?" Caesar asked.

"Well, I don't know. I can't think of anything for you to do. I don't like working my guests, that's not me. Umm, let me think about it. You just enjoy yourself. Watch some television. Listen to the radio. Read the newspaper. I'll let you know if I need you." Mr. Scott walked to the garage where he occupied his mechanic business.

Scanning the living room, Caesar noticed a collection of newspapers that were sorted by date and year. They were a series of newspapers of foreign and domestic events. Some of the newspapers dated back to the

1920s and 1940s, significant years when the countries attention shifted from World War II, and the impact of the Great Depression and racism. The newspapers had valuable information about stories of wars, lynching of blacks in the south, invasions of World War II and Pearl Harbor, the shape of America and the direction it was heading, and the black struggle in America, a place that instituted segregation and economic instability.

President Franklin D. Roosevelt delivered a speech on January 6, 1941, in which he declared that all people were entitled to freedom of speech, worship, which became a famous speech.

Addressing members of the 77th Congress, President Roosevelt caught the eyes and ears of Americans, as well as blacks during the time of segregation in the United States. Caesar analyzed President Roosevelt's speech and applied the president's speech to his own life and community.

Analyzing the Spirituality of a Victory

The three important rhythms to the beating drum are approach, influence, and support.

The foundation to the beating drum is the essential transformation of equality, inspiration, and faith within its own right. Building a foundation of testimony is done through strength by acknowledging that faith is a conscious thought. Applying the drum to our daily lives, there can be a fundamental formation of essential human freedoms. The drum of the essential guide is a gift that we all can use to build a foundation of equality, inspiration, and faith for our families and ourselves within its own right.

The pillar drums of the essential guide are the fruitful seeds, intensive transformation, and the central guide of family and community structure. The beating drum is the transformation in the community inspiring family determination without bias in the home and community.

Faithfully take an oath to become involved in the community. Inspiring children and adults is the determination to have a vision and a dream. One has to be committed to planning his or her future and must have a positive attitude of ethics, honesty, and integrity to keep families secure and safe. The satisfaction of strength comes from the things that have been done to make its people conscious of family and community. This is to have faith with conscious and to observe the evidence of humanity and cultural advantage. Furthermore, what a family builds shall not live by someone else's deceitful commands. Applying the beating drum to one's daily life, there can be a fundamental foundation of the three essential human freedoms. The first is having a desire to speak with expression. Second, for one to have the chance to restore freedom to think. The third is having the freedom from want...one can strengthen financial stability in the family.

The evidence of the cultural disadvantaged is spiritually overcoming the complexity of social injustice and seeking and creating a safe environment.

The complexity of social crisis is not a separate problem within the black community; it is of all social behavior of all ethnic groups and societies.

The courage to treat mental disadvantage in the black community doesn't just focus on ethnic groups, societies, and communities it also includes family.

The disadvantage of the social crisis is it hasn't focus its attention among the black community. This disadvantage; the negro has inherited social justice and equality.

The goal is to move forward and recede from the social crisis of cultural disadvantage. Without moving forward, the exploitation of the blacks will be denied cultural freedom.

The obstacles and struggles for cultural freedom have been the challenges to move forward.

It is never simple or easy to build a testimony of strength and process that is historic within its own right. When losing the spiritual faith in God, the freedom for cultural advantage is lost.

CHAPTER 32
TRAVELING CAN BRAND A PERSON

It was weeks Caesar living with the Scotts, for driving him out of Tennessee would be a risk, for tension was rising in protest for better public schools for children, the segregation of colleges, blacks being denied jobs, blacks being lynched and killed by the Klan. Racism in the South and throughout the country was driving the journey to an American dream to its tipping point.

"I've been reading the newspapers. I noticed you keep up on current events," Caesar said. Mr. Scott mentioned to Caesar to read Executive Order 8802 an important executive order signed by President Roosevelt in 1941.

The telephone rang. Mrs. Scott answered the call. On the other end…was Parker. His wife had gone into labor, and he would be unable to make it to work. Mr. Scott would be short-handed for that day and possibility for the whole week.

"Can you teach me?" Caesar asked. Mr. Scott rubbed his forehead and gazed a look at his wife. She gave him a nod, agreeing with his question to Mr. Scott. "I guess so. Sitting around the house isn't gonna do you any good. Come on, Caesar," Mr. Scott responded.

Mr. Scott began giving Caesar a quick lesson on correct tools tuning vehicle…

"You're a fast learner," Mr. Scott said, surprised at Caesar's fast learning and capability.

The car shop was now open as cars arrived for servicing.

Assisting Mr. Scott, Caesar went out of his way to clean the customer's windows after servicing their vehicles. His generosity came with a tip for his kind greetings and cleanliness. Caesar felt he had done his best.

Sitting at the dinner table, Mr. and Mrs. Scott praised Caesar for his initiative to help in the garage.

"Tomorrow, I'm gonna to teach you another skill," Mr. Scott said.

"Before I forget." He handed Caesar twenty-five dollars for helping him in the garage.

"You earned it, and you worked hard," Mr. Scott said with proudness.

"Thank you, sir," Caesar said, folded his hands in prayer.

Mr. Scott was not much of a television person. He and his wife Thelma were more interested in politics and history. Mr. Scott and Caesar talked about slavery, the reconstruction period, World War I, and World War II—

Mr. Scott furthered the discussion on detailing of the Civil War, and when war became imminent and slaves joined the Confederate Army. The slave men were told that if they fought for the Confederate Army, they would become freedmen.

After blacks had enlisted in the Confederate Army, they would not be allowed to fight. Black slaves who had joined the Confederate Army were either a laborer or a body servant, and became instrumental for building railroads and working in coalmines. As tension of the Civil War began to grow after 1861, the large number of casualties became a reality of the Civil War.

In the state of Maryland, six black military regiments were formed to fight in the Civil War.

Over eight thousand enslaved men played a role in the military, war strategies, and winning the Civil War. The 36th U.S. Colored Infantry guarded the Confederate prison at Point Lookout, Maryland.

Mrs. Scott began telling the story of her ancestors. The divide and argument in Chesapeake was over freeing black slaves.

During the beginning of the Civil War in 1861, enslaved men and women seized the opportunity to escape slavery in the South.

Part of Mr. and Mrs. Scott's collection of events were articles of laws that forbad interracial marriage in the Northern and Southern states. Mr. Scott and his wife moved to Tennessee after wedding in Kentucky—

Three days after the birth of his daughter, Parker returned to work. Mr. Scott could at that point teach Caesar how to draft. However, teaching him drafting would be done after dinner.

The garage is where Mr. Scott did all of his work, including drafting and painting.

A dim light beamed of the drafting board, this is where Mr. Scott did all of his company business, except counting his daily earnings.

With some clear drafting paper, a protractor, pencil, ruler, and an eraser, Mr. Scott showed Caesar how to draw irregular curves, circles, squares, and triangles.

"Good. Good," Mr. Scott said looking over Caesar's shoulder.

"I need more practice," Caesar said. Mr. Scott assured that his drafting would come in time.

The next morning, Caesar received news from Mr. Parker that his travel to St. Louis, Missouri would be safe, for his aunt was waiting for him—

Christmas day was approaching, for the Scotts and Parkers had families in Kansas, and it would be the perfect time to travel.

Mr. Scott drove while Parker sat in the front passenger seat. Sitting in the back was Caesar, along with Mrs. Scott, Parker wife Ann and their newborn baby.

Finally, Caesar made it to his destination, for traveling can brand a person to adjust to lessons learned.

Aunt Estella stood at the front door waiting for Caesar's arrival. With open arms, she gave Caesar a hug. "I take it your travel to get here wasn't so friendly?" Aunt Estella said.

"Aunt Estella, we all come to live with some authentic fear. Faith is more reliable than being in fear," Caesar bluntly acclaimed.

"I don't know how you do it," Aunt Estella hand raised praising to the blue skies.

"A nice man named Tom Carter and his family hid me...I stayed with Mr. and Mrs. Scott, these two generous folks." With greetings from his aunt and Mr. and Mrs. Scott, and Parker and Ann, she invited them in the house. The stay was not long, for they had to drive to the state of Kansas.

"You have an intelligent nephew," Mr. Scott said. The generous gesture from Mr. Scott left a vibrate smile on Aunt Estella's face.

After a brief visit, the Scotts and the Parkers said their goodbyes to Caesar, his aunt Estella, and her husband.

Caesar was excited to be with his relatives.

"Where's Uncle Richard?" Caesar asked.

Caesar never knew Uncle Richard, for it would be the first time meeting his father's brother. Uncle Richard was a hardworking man who lived without fear.

With knowledge of family history, he would tell anyone who would listen. However, he had taking ill and his health was failing fast.

"Your father's brother is ailing. I don't know how much time he has left, but you better make use of what he has left," Aunt Estella said sadly holding back tears.

Thorne guarded the entrance to his master's bedroom, while his master lay comfortably in bed.

"Hi, Uncle Richard," Caesar said in a low voice, slowly walking to his bed.

"Whose child are you?" Uncle Richard asked in a weak voice.

"I'm Dingus's son, Caesar."

"Caesar! Come on in! Grab a chair next to me," Uncle Richard responded with a bright, but weak smile.

"Your siblings are here—I don't care for them too much—I don't know why they came to see me," Uncle Richard said.

"How so?" Caesar asked curiously.

"They too afraid to look at death. I don't know where they got their thinking from. I think it was that wild story my father would tell the grandchildren," Uncle Richard said trying to catch his breath.

"I don't know the story Uncle Richard. Grandfather Charles II, never told me," Caesar said, scratching his chin.

Uncle Richard coughed weakly, "You probably don't remember the story. Can you bring me a cup of tea?" Uncle Richard asked softly speaking.

"Yes, Uncle Richard." In the kitchen on the stove sat a hot teapot.

He poured a cup of tea for Uncle Richard. Walking back to Uncle Richard's bedroom, he saw Becky in the living room. She saw he was strong and preserved.

"I know what you did, Becky. I want my death certificate. I need to prove that I am alive," Caesar said angrily.

"I don't have it. It's in Los Angeles," Becky's voice crackled.

"Well, when I get to Los Angeles…you betta have it," Caesar responded with aggression, pointing his finger at her.

Not giving Becky a time to respond, he walked toward the entrance of the bedroom door where Thorne welcomed him, Becky and Ellen followed him into the bedroom, Thorne growled loudly.

Sitting in the doorway to Uncle Richard's bedroom, Thorne exercised his territory toward Becky and Ellen.

"Thorne, won't let no's one in the room to see's Uncle Richard," Becky said, shyly. After Thorne settled down from growling, he gracefully walked over to Caesar.

"Well, maybe he's tired of seeing too many faces. Come back later, when Thorne's feeling better." Uncle Richard did not care to be in the company of his nieces—to say the least.

Caesar stroked Thorne's beautiful brown and gold coat, by his request. Thorne enjoyed the soft comfort of Caesar's hand massaging, his thick skin, and his silky texture coat.

Uncle Richard and Caesar reminisced about the old days growing up in the south, and his brother Dingus.

CHAPTER 33
PASSAGE: UNIVERSAL VALUES

The pain came and went for Uncle Richard as his body became weaker.

Caesar listened carefully, as Uncle Richard told the history of the family. Speaking in a low voice, the crackling and gargle of his words was soft and broken.

"Hand me the Bible," Uncle Richard said, pointing to his black Bible opened to Psalm 23 that lay opened on his dresser. Caesar handed him the open Bible.

"Lo, children are an heritage of the LORD: and the fruit of the womb is his reward. As arrows are in the hand of a mighty man; so are children of the youth. Happy is the man that hath his quiver full

174

of them: they shall not be ashamed, but they shall speak with the enemies in the age."

—Psalm 127:3-5.

Uncle Richard gave the Bible back to him, and in a soft voice he explained, "The Bible has no limits. Life has no limits. The passage of the Bible is the beating drum that examines our life with no limits. What you have in your hand is the external victory and the internal spirit of Christ Jesus who is in God. How does God want you to look at your trials and failures in life? This is how; I want you to look at it, life is without limits. We may have horrible things; bad things happen to us in life, but strength can keep us alive. The beast can distract us; he will darken our perception and disorder our sacred abode. The *salesman*. We only have one life. We only let life limit our ideas and passions in life, if we let others control our purpose in life. You have to believe in the Lord's faith, from your heart," Uncle Richard pointing to the ceiling and continued, "our Lord and Savior Christ Jesus, knows who his true believers are. I bet you saw him several times in your life and didn't know it. Never limit yourself to others," Uncle Richard explained.

The movement of Uncle Richard's hands and arms was slow and weak, as he waited patiently for his time to come. The energy between him and Caesar was rich and spiritual.

Feeding his energy to Uncle Richard would last through the coming days and nights.

"Are you ready to eat dinner Uncle Richard?" Caesar asked.

"Yes, Caesar," Uncle Richard replied, weakly. Caesar walked into the kitchen. He piled his dinner plate with baked turkey, dressing, vegetables, and a glass of orange juice that his aunt made. He returned to Uncle Richards's bedroom.

"I'm not a big eater like I used to be," Uncle Richard continued, "give the rest to Thorne. He'll eat it."

"Will you be eating dinner?" Uncle Richard asked.

"Yes sir, but I'm not hungry right now." Cutting the baked turkey in small portions, and with a fork, he slowly feeds his uncle.

He waited patiently for his hand to command him to continue feeding him while resting between servings.

Walking over from Estella's house, "There's too much noise over there," Aunt Emma said tiredly.

After feeding Uncle Richard, Caesar excused himself from his uncle's bedside. He motioned for Aunt Emma to sit with her ailing brother-in-law. She was the second person Thorne accepted near his master.

"How are you Caesar? Aunt Emma asked after visiting her brother-in-law. Aunt Emma continued, "I heard about your accident back in Louisiana." He told her the story of that stormy night.

"What in the tarnation was your mother thinking? With all those bad kids of Naomi. They are some spoil apples," Aunt Emma said, angrily. He sat and listened to Emma complain about his brothers and sisters, as well as Lucy. His mind quickly drifted left.

"I have family secrets to tell you," Aunt Emma said. She knew that it would be senseless to tell his siblings and other distant relatives the family secret. Offering her his seat, he quickly pulled up a chair next to her, both sipping on a hot cup of coffee.

Uncle Richard was resting comfortably in his bed asleep. While sitting near the doorway of his master's bedroom, Thorne's ears and eyes were wide open, waiting to hear the family secrets. She read the letter to Caesar that her brother Dingus had written to her.

"Promise me that you won't say anything to your brothers and sisters about this letter," Aunt Emma said.

"I promise…" Caesar maturely explained.

"Take good care of yourself," Aunt Emma said. After she had told Caesar the family secrets, she walked back to Estella's house.

Caesar saw Uncle Richard well rested in bed. He drifted off asleep in a chair that sat next Uncle Richard. The next morning, he realized that he had slept through the entire night.

Walking toward the window outside stood an old tree in the front yard. He noticed a reflection of a person at the window.

Caesar turned his body around quickly.

There Uncle Richard lay, rested and asleep. Thorne stood next to Caesar scratching his long paws against his pants.

He walked over to Uncle Richard's bed to touch his forehead—soaks a cold washcloth, placing it on his feet.

There was no movement from Uncle Richard.

Uncle Richard was at rest and peace. He walked over to his aunt's house with the news of Richard Sweeney's death.

Aunt Estella and her husband walked to Uncle Richard's house to confirm of his passing.

An uncle, Caesar never knew, but for the short time, he had the opportunity to know his uncle's words of wisdom and courage. Knowing a person for a few moments can give words of universal values.

Richard Sweeney's funeral was held at a Baptist Church located not too far from Crystal, Missouri. Caesar's brothers and sisters sat near the back rows of the church while, Lucy, aunts, uncles, other family friends, and Caesar sat in the front and middle rows in the church.

There was the sound of chanting coming from Ellen's daughter Brenda that gave uneasy thoughts among the grieving mourners. The distracting chanting sounds coming from Brenda was her attempt to revoke the spirit.

"Don't turn around," Aunt Estella said, sitting next to Caesar. He could not help himself, making a quick glance at the person sitting in the row behind him. He turned back around.

The chanting sounds became louder as Brenda rocks back in forth in her seat. With sweat rolling down the pastor's face, he preached the gospel of II Timothy. Brenda screamed out a piercing cry, loudly.

Aunt Estella got the preacher's attention. "Speed it up," she silently whispered to him.

Relieved to be standing outside the church, mourners whispered to each other questioning, who was the annoying person chanting in the second row of the church?

"Caesar, who in tarnation was that making all that noise?" Aunt Emma asked.

"It was the daughter of Ellen," He responded.

"Her one and only child, Becky. Oh my Lord. To each his own," Aunt Emma shaking her head and smoothing out the patterns of the arm wickless of her dress.

Lucy approached Caesar with open arms, she was happy to see her son alive and well.

Aunt Emma decided to attend with the other mourners, while Lucy and Caesar spent time alone.

"Caesar, why don't you come backs to Los Angeles with us?" He smelled the liquor on her breath as she spoke to him.

He was not happy with the hard liquor that stale on her breath.

"Umm…No—" Caesar responded. Naomi disrupted quietly, leaning next to Lucy. "Ms. Sweeney, you knows there's not 'nough room at home for him," she said.

Lucy gave a half chuckle, thinking what to say next. It was clear that Naomi's poison of lies had guided his mother away from her son; her children's impatience to quilt a better life for themselves. Caesar remembered Paul and the *salesman*. He was to be the successor to his father, for this the poison words cast upon the Sweeney family will have a cost, but not just yet.

"Becky is one of the eldest child in family. She can make the decisions…" Naomi reminded Lucy and smiling with poise.

The poison liquor controlled his mother, and his siblings' mind and faith; and that Naomi loved.

After the funeral of Uncle Richard, Caesar decided to stay with his aunt and her husband for a while, for he was not ready leave Missouri behind.

Sitting on the front porch, watching the stars' glitter in the night sky, He dwelled on the loss of antiquity, good and bad memories.

Becky looked up to Naomi with several attempts to carbon copy Naomi's potion of lies. Becky was the boss to her younger siblings whenever she could be. When Dingus was alive, he had warned his children about Naomi, more often forewarned Becky and Ellen.

Lucy would find herself taking her husband's side. However, after the death of Dingus, Lucy could not resist what Naomi was giving, that was fantasy of tricky and lies.

"Caesar, come inside and eat some of this good Gumbo," Becky said bossily.

"I'll be right in." Everyone loved Becky's cooking and her most popular dish, Gumbo.

Caesar took a sip of the Gumbo juice...

"What the hell is this tar pit, ghastly...This gumbo juice is horrible," Caesar muttered. He continued, "Mom never fixed Gumbo like this before."

The gumbo had been too extended, the color of the coffee color roux was muddy black, and with the one shrimp hiding in the recipe, it struggled back up to the top for air. The idea of good gumbo is a roux color, a dark reddish-brown color.

CHAPTER 34
FAINT HEARTED
I'M A 'GONNA BIRD

In August 1947, with one piece of luggage in his hand, Caesar took the Greyhound bus to Los Angeles, California to be with his family. While traveling to Los Angeles, and on occasions, white and black passengers spoke about their comings and goings…

As the bus travels through the night, his thoughts were on what strength his family would need to quilt their path in life, and that the Faint Hearted: I'm A 'Gonna Bird can only lead the weak and the insecure…This bird is difficult to identify because it blends easily into most backgrounds.

Unless one uses powerful glasses, one has to get close up with keen observation and much use one can learn to recognize it handily.

A person can be repeatedly taken in by this bird, mostly through a common fault of all ages, which is a distraction and innocence, coupled with the desire that most people have to believe in their fellow creature.

Mostly, patience and a sense of humor are needed when in direct contact with the I'm A 'Gonna Bird, for its way of changing shapes and colors can be misleading. It's most productive use to humanity is to serve as a horrible example. The I'm A 'Gonna Bird can best be spotted by the word games; it plays, and that it has the ability to tell pretty, but showy pictures of its intentions. This serves to mask its true intentions and interests.

The 'I'm A 'Gonna accomplishments are largely invisible. That is, they speak of themselves…can never produce any tangible results, their expertise lies in fair promises of dreams that can be odd at times. It does this by reciting in a strident voice the many wrongs done to it during its lifetime.

One can observe that when this happens, the bird resorts to severe forms of dissolution or physical action, being weak in resolve, plus incapable of long periods of concentration. The bird willpower soon gives way to unpreparedness and self-doubt, which can be easily understood when observing that it starts with no clear plans. Its efforts were doomed to failure from the outset.

Part of the I'm A 'Gonna Bird's camouflage is…relentless criticism of other birds' efforts, and unfortunates…

When the tables of assessment are turned the I'm A 'Gonna Bird retreats into rationalizing its faults and distributes its failures to its mate, relatives, friends, and society in general. *The salesman...*

This is self-delusion, and at the same time serve to deceive and mislead a less observant person. One other queer trait this bird has is that a person can be considered an asset. It's an ability to demonstrate a variety of back handed kindnesses. Sometimes this is one out of utter loneliness or a deep desire to be accepted by other birds.

However, when their passive acceptance is not demonstrated in the manner that the I'm A 'Gonna Bird expects, it causes serious frustration and confusion, which only adds to its further isolation. In this way, it resembles the Dodo bird...The *salesman.*

Part of the I'm A 'Gonna Bird's problem can be traced to its first rejection by its parents.

Being self-centered, this species tends to abandon its young at an early age, and this trait of rejection is normally inherited.

The mating of the bird, it seems, is only to preserve the species.

It is never a lasting relationship. The I'm A 'Gonna is a very odd bird, but quite harmless when compared with some of the other feathered families.

CHAPTER 35

PILLAR

Arriving in Los Angeles, California in the early evening, Caesar hitched a ride to his mother's house and on his arrival, he heard the voice of Becky fussing over space in the kitchen.

Standing in the doorway was Naomi's brother Bill. Caesar greeted Bill with a friendly wave.

"I hate you," Bill responded with an unexpected gesture of angry words. However, Caesar would not allow the words from Bill make him weak. Bill did not like the idea that Caesar was forewarning his family of his sister. He was greeted with hugs and joy from his mother and siblings.

Time passed fast; it was late, and Naomi's children had to turn in for bed for an early rise for Sunday school.

Caesar struggled to get comfortable on the couch, fighting to stay awake. He drifted off to sleep—

There was a thought of a young boy running fast across an open field.

The sun sprinkles the tall grass; his hands brush the tips of the grass as his playful mind enjoys the sun. His body is not tired from the strain of running across the grass with joy.

A dark-gray wolf with shiny white claws appears. A pack of wolves follows behind the leading wolf, as he glares into the boy's eyes. The boy was not afraid of the wolves, but it was in his best interest not to follow the pack of wolves, but to walk away—

"Pu' the greens on the stove. Put the greens on the stove," a voice said repeatedly. Caesar was awakened. He adjusted his eyes from an incomplete dream, to find his mother sitting in her rocking chair, sipping on a cup of hot tea.

"Good mornin' Caesar," Lucy said, rubbing her shoulder. Caesar replied with a good morning greeting.

Standing in the doorway to the kitchen, Becky offered her mother another cup of tea.

"Caesar, you gonna have to clear this area. Kids be gettin' up soon," Becky said quickly. Naomi's children were the center attention of the Sweeney family and the youngest son Adam. She continued, "You suppos' to be dead," Becky said, her jaw tightened with anger. Naomi's poison of words would dictate the Sweeney family. Naomi had won the crown to rule the Sweeney family, but she did not conquer the battle to rule Caesar.

He went outside to catch a breath of fresh air while Naomi's kids cluttered the living room. After Naomi prepared her children for Sunday school in the morning, she struggled to keep up with them while walking to church. Caesar thought it would be safe to enter the house after Naomi, and her children left the house. Sniffing and investigating a sweet liquid substance he had smelt coming from his mother's teacup, he noticed, the smell was not a hot tea, but a strong liquor his father used to forbid in the house. He walked over to where his mother had her teacup and smelled Bourbon on her breath.

"Caesar, you can't stay here...There's not 'nough room fore you. Maybe you cans stays with your cousin. He lives downs the street," Lucy said, sipping from her teacup. Naomi had found a way to control his mother and her children. With Lucy's finances, Naomi would control with greed and poisoned plans.

"Mother, you should be making the decisions... Naomi is not blood," Caesar said on the break of tears; he continued, "she will destroy the family, and this will be a tragedy to the family. The suffering will not just be on you, but also your children. This will be a disaster for the Sweeney family. I can't tell you or Becky, or any of my brothers and sisters what to do, but I can guide the family in the right direction." He has seen the grave of the world, the teaching of antiquity.

Naomi's destruction would not be the last warning to his family.

He made an appeal to his mother and siblings.

"Our father fought whole-heartedly to keep this family together. Naomi will ruin what Daddy had fought hard to save—that was our strength within ourselves and each other," Caesar said, paused for a second.

"A day will come when the drum will stop beating. The drum will no longer sound. You will be paying the pipe piper," Caesar said, impatiently.

"Naomi's a good person. You left us. You left yore family," Lucy said, with cracking in her voice, holding back tears.

"What are you talking about?" It had come to Caesar's attention that his mother was unaware of what evil thing Becky had done.

"…I don't want to talk about this no more, Caesar," Lucy cried.

He tried pleading with his mother.

"Listen to me. Naomi is controlling, and she will ruin the Sweeney family. What she's giving you will not last forever. That liquor she's feeding you is poison. I'm warning y'all to stay away from Naomi's poisonous mind. She is going to destroy Henry. She is going to destroy everything around you…Your family, your children, their husbands, and their wives," Caesar said, ripping the sweat from his face.

Caesar's warning to his mother and his siblings would be an opinion they would not accept. The evil bird of greed and poisonous words would be the blind mother and her children—

As a tradition, Sundays were always family day for the Sweeney family. The reuniting of family memories and photos would be shared with uncles, aunts, and cousins, and would be the passing of stories that would last a lifetime. In addition, Los Angeles, California would become the residing home for most of the Sweeney family and their extended relatives.

Later in the afternoon, after everyone had eaten dinner, relatives went about their way, leaving the house a mess. The cleaning detail consisted of Stella washing dishes in the kitchen, Sarah collecting liquor bottles and cans scattered in the living room. However, Becky found a way to escape cleaning detail, sipping on a tall glass of ice tea and watching Naomi's children play joyfully in the backyard.

In the dining room, Naomi found a way to pick an argument with Henry.

Caesar gazed out the living room window, adjusting his thoughts. He thought of ways to try to save his family from Naomi. Maybe there's was a way.

Late Sunday evening turned into night, as the rain began to fall in Los Angeles.

The dark clouds rolled against the skies connecting and piecing together the different puzzle of clouds. The beam of lightning flashes the city's innocents.

"Now, that you have found us, and we have taken a look at you, you can go on back to where ever you came from… We don't want any sick people around here," Uncle Scott said, standing in the doorway that led to living room. Lucy did not object to her brother's remark to Caesar.

For a moment, Caesar's soul weakened from the lash of cold words from his uncle. It would be a battle he would not win, for the family. He was blamed for failing at his responsibilities to secure his family and there would be no sympathy for Caesar. His health and sickness would not be a reality that his family would accept. His challenges he would have to face, alone.

Only those that have absorbed life, and tolerated man can learn something about his humanity at that time.

The storm finally passed, and the sky restored its presence to the earth. Lucy fell asleep in her rocking chair, with an empty teacup sitting next to her on a small console table.

Caesar gives his mother a goodbye kiss on her forehead. He thought it would be safe to leave, for he must move on with his life. Path for the hunger for knowledge, life, and humanity.

There was the sound of inspiring words coming from the house of worshiping. "Howbeit when he, the Spirit of truth, is come, he will guide you into all truth: for he shall not speak of himself; but whatsoever he shall hear, that shall he speak; and he will shew you things to come. He shall glorify me; for he shall receive of mine, and shall shew it unto you. All things that the Father hath are mine: therefore said I, that he shall take of mine, and shall shew it unto you."

— John: 16:13-15.

In the house of the Lord, he hears the voices' singing. The choir shout repeatedly: He is…The melody of words of a male tenor voice singing:

> You can't change my mind,
> With joy, I praise Him,
> With wood and of earth soil.

> The drum.
> He the pillar.
> He the victory.

For the rules to restore and preserve humanity are simple. The thirst of determination and the reality of life is a strand of humanity:

> You can't change my mind,
> I ask him for mercy.
> He gave me charity and advice;
> He breaks the chains of our pain.

> He led me out of the cave,
> Back to reality.
> He is a beautiful God.

Lucy opened her eyes and screamed after having a nightmare. Sobering up from the hard liquor…

"Where's Caesar?" Lucy asked, with a puzzled look on her face.

"He gone momma," Stella said.

Lucy ran out the front door barefooted.

"Caesar!" Lucy yelled. She screamed out to the night with cries and despair.

She heard the voices from the house of the Lord, but she was in doubt.

"CAESAR!" Lucy screamed, again. He was anointed by the words.

The drum.
He the pillar.
He the victory.

His hands made my clay of victories.
He patches my scars with a strength.
Field with vessels of divine and fruit;
He is a Pillar Drum.

He gave me salvation,
When I went down in battle.
He is a Pillar Drum.
He breaks every chain our tribulations.

He restored my faith,
When I thought I went down in defeat;
He had put my feet back on solid ground.

He will piece you back together again;
He is a Victory Drum.

If you believe in the Lord's words;
He will not let you down;

He gives only good advice;
He is a faithful God.
He gives us hope with no limits.
He gives us voices of pillars with no limits;
He is a Pillar Drum.

"Where are you, CAESAR," Lucy screamed.

The dark and cold air pierced her body; she continued her desperate cry for her son.

"COME BACK! CAESAR." She collapsed down on her knees dug in the earth's soil, with her hands covering her face. As the tears rolled down her face, her ears were numb. The choir repeated to the blind, He is…

He's never far away,
Each time when I stumble,
Misery and pain,
I shout the Lord's name.

He rescues us from our trials,
With open arms;
He will give his salvation.
He shelters his children with love.

I shout out his name,
Lord, Help Me,

And I then say,
He is a Pillar God.

My pillar!
My pillar!
My pillar!

He is…
He is…

He is a Pillar of a Victory Beating Drum.

Caesar was too far away from home to hear his mother's cry.

God walks with us through thick and thin, stormy days, dark nights, death, the light of internal life, the beating drum. Voice of our faith is our trust in God.

Unconditionally, our drum, we all have been forewarned, and unconditionally by our ancestors. He sacrificed his life, our courage is to trust God without limits. Our life, we are defenseless without him. Our weakness, we are defenseless when we are strong, and our trials that are unconditional and defenseless is the response to the beating drum. The drum is beating hard enough, the drum always beats loud, the Lord all these years, holds the essence of our trials, and strengths. The pillar of strength, the victory all tribulations, the beating of all trials, and the drum of all shields.

EPILOGUE
PSALM 23

"The Lord is my shepherd; I shall not want. He maketh me to lie down in green pastures: he leadeth me beside the still waters. He restoreth my soul: he leadeth me in the paths of righteousness for his name's sake. Yea, though I walk through the valley of the shadow of death, I will fear no evil: for Thou art with me; Thy rod the Thy staff they comfort me. Thou preparest a table before me in the presence of mine enemies: Thou annointest my head with oil; my cup runneth over. Surely goodness and mercy shall follow me

all the days of my life; and I will dwell
in the house of the LORD for ever."

—Psalm 23

⊷ ⊶

Life Reflections of Cesar Swiney

Cesar received his formal education in the public schools of Clarks, Louisiana.

Cesar later moved to California, where he received his GED and later attended college. Quite proficient with his hands, Cesar learned and mastered many skills, including architecture, agriculture, drafting, painting, photography, wood work, and gardening... In many ways Cesar's talent was to create ideas in life. The ability to challenge himself to learn crafting and workmanship lasted a life time and was memorable. God allowed him to rebuild with his own bare hands, the house he purchased for his wife in 1964.

A passionate learner, he studied history and auto mechanics. He loved golfing and fishing; and he loved his Ford F150 truck. Cesar was named Commander-in-Chief Santa Monica Consistory #296, 33 degree, on October 15, 1995. Cesar was loving, kind, friendly, and an outspoken father, who worked hard at what he did in life-his job, and taking care of his wife and children-. He passed a month before his seventy-seventh birthday in June 2001.

GENEALOGY PART 1

In 1983, Maryalice Swiney-Zoë began helping her father Cesar Swiney to bring about a genealogy of the Swiney family ancestors. The research for family history...turned into the story of her father's life. The research project consisted of oral and written documents and photographs of the Swiney family.

Most importantly, as a child, Swiney-Zoë inherited Charles Swiney II, her great grandfather's journal.

She examined and analyzed the journal, translating recording entries in the journal that her great-grand father and her grandfather had written. The journal also included records from purchases made between 1918 and 1934 and other significant journal entries.

The journal also included the letter codes written by her father. Her father taught her how to read some of the codes, but not all the written codes. This is where she discovered that her father was telling his story as a

197

child in codes. For decades, Swiney-Zoë studied and examined the letter codes written by her father and her African ancestors.

Swiney-Zoë began studying the oral and written documents of her ancestors in order to write the story of her father's childhood into adulthood.

Charles II was described as being a light-skinned mulatto. He grew into adulthood living on the Mr. Mason's large farm, and sharecropping sections of the farm. During Civil War, there arose disputes over sharecropping land and sometimes these disputes became brutal.

The Civil War in 1865 and the failure of sharecropping, a treaty industry structure was formed. The treaty industry structure was contracted between whites, and blacks to restore sharecropping land. The treaty failed to reform whites and blacks to work together to restore an economic solution to the sharecropping industry. The Freedmen's Bureau was a contracting system between the former slaves and sharecropping land that was owned by the whites.

The contracting system resulted in the failure of conducting business both between white and black farmers. Some states allow freed slaves to own sharecropped land, other freed slaves returned sharecropped land to its original owners.

After becoming a young man, Charles II fell in love with a young woman by the name Lucie Morris, born 1860, who lived on an adjoining sharecropping farm in

Georgia. With permission from slave master Charles Sweeney, Charles Sweeney II and Lucie Morris would marry in 1879 and they continued sharecropping. Lucie had a sister name Phoebe born 1859.

By now, Charles II had succeeded in buying a section of land, where he would begin raising his family in Georgia.

Charles II and his wife Lucie Morris birthed six children, William born 1879, Charles III born 1888. In 1896, Charles II and his wife Lucie moved to Louisiana, where they had five more children, a set of twins, Dingus and his twin brother Rush born 1895, Estella 1897, Rosie born 1899, and Richard born 1900.

In 1901, there had been a dispute over cotton and land in Louisiana. As a result, there was the lynching of Charles III, and his brother William was sent to prison. William was later released from prison and was helped to escape from Louisiana to Mississippi by sympathetic whites.

William was helped to escape by a white man who had owned a boat; the owner of the boat hired two other white men to help row the boat across the Mississippi. During William's escape out of Louisiana, he was struck over the head with an oar by one the rowers and was knocked overboard. As the owner lost control of the boat, the swift water began to ascend the boat.

The sympathetic white man managed to hold William by his shirt and pull him back to the boat; this way William could hold on until they reached the west shore. There was a confrontation between the two white men.

As the two men fought, the man who had instigated the throwing of the oar was confronted and killed. William was pulled to safety were the three men eventually settled the boat in Mississippi. William was told to run and hide. William and the white man traveled with a wagon train, heading towards Alabama. The wagon master guided the two men in what direction to travel, for he knew of a small-town where blacks lived among sympathetic whites in Georgia.

The two men took the wagon master's advice; William reunited with his parents and siblings in a small town in Georgia.

GENEALOGY PART 2

The "Bonner" was one of the several agriculture plantations and farming industry in the United States. In Hancock, Georgia "Bonner" farm was a plantation, where free slaves worked as farmers and eventually owning a portion of the farming land.

There was a high demand for cotton, as well as wheat, oats, and vegetables on the "Bonner" farm. Cesar Brown married a woman named Kathleen.

Cesar and his wife Kathleen had the opportunity to buy and become owners of a section of the "Bonner" farm. The Brown family had ten children; their names were Lucy born in 1894, Larlue born 1896, Rodger born 1898, Sip born 1900, Williams born 1902, Lilly born 1904, Betty born 1906, Emma born 1908, Mamie born 1910; and Scott born 1912.

After the passing of the father Cesar Brown and later the mother Kathleen Brown, the son William marries and moves with his wife to Festus, Missouri. William's wife has a daughter named Estella "Dale" and later having a son name Rodger. In 1913, Dingus and his twin brother Rush Swiney continued to farm in Georgia.

Dingus and his twin brother were both employed not too far from the "Bonner" farm. Dingus Swiney wooed and won the love of his life, a young woman who resided on the large "Bonner" farm name Lucy Brown. He soon married Lucy in a small town in Georgia. Dingus twin brother Rush married the other sister Larlue.

THE JOURNAL LEDGER

Talking over with his twin brother Rush the financial difficulties both families were having, both Dingus and Rush decided to look for another line of work, one that would earn them regular salaries, they both sorely needed.

Before moving their families to Louisiana, Dingus and Rush worked three jobs, to save enough money to make their move to Louisiana. Dingus and Charles II kept a detail journal between the years 1918 and 1934 of their finances. The entries in the journal were purchases, profits...entries written by Dingus and Charles II. Before and during the Great Depression, there is keen insight of how families struggled to survive. Items recorded in the journal while living Georgia is as follows, in 1918, there was a purchase of one hog, one dollar, another purchase one hog, sixty-nine cents. One large hog one dollar and sixteen cents. Another hog purchased eighty-four cents.

In the winter of 1918, Charles Swiney II became the owner of livestock that was used for slaughtering; this is how the family survived.

The journal began in 1918, a diary sales transactions of goods and services. Charles II bought four bolts, thirty cents. Twenty pounds of salt; cornmeal twenty pounds, one dollar; snuff, twenty-five cents; coffee, ten pounds one dollar; two gallons of syrup, two dollars and twenty cents. Sacks of oats how many not recorded, for seven dollars. These are just a few of listings found in the journal. Dingus received these prices for his products, in for the year of 1920. The first bale, five dollars. The second bale, five dollars. He sold the third bale, five dollars. The fourth bale five dollars. The fifth bale, four dollars.

He earned that particular month from selling bale, twenty-four dollars...The total earning for the year 1920 was fifty dollars. For the year in 1921, he received money for the selling of bales. First bale, he received five dollars. The second bale five dollars. Three bales, five dollars. His profit in the year 1921 was fifteen dollars. This was discouraging time for him, but, by now, Dingus was more determined than ever to leave the farming industry. At last, by working extra hard, Dingus and his brother Rush managed to save enough money needed, moving from Georgia to Louisiana. Dingus Swiney paid taxes. A state tax ninety-five cents. Good improved roads, four cents. A Parish tax in Richmond, one dollar and sixty cents. A school tax one dollar and thirty cents. That year he bought his wife a new coat, paying fifteen dollars.

POST A TRIUMPH AND DEFEAT A BARREL

A PILLAR OF A VICTORY BEATING DRUM

Maryalice Swiney-Zoe

Jungle Boogie Ink

ABOUT THE AUTHOR

Maryalice Swiney-Zoë was born and raised in Los Angeles, California by her parents Cesar and Doll Swiney. At the age of five, she began taking piano lessons. She caught on quickly, reading and writing piano music by the age of nine. For ten years, she continued her passion for playing the piano by playing in several piano recitals in Los Angeles. When she was in the first grade, she had her first experience with politics. She had the opportunity to meet the Edmund Gerald "Jerry" Brown Jr. sister Kathleen Brown.

At the age of ten, she learned sign language and sang in the junior choir. Later in her teenage years, she learned to read and play the violin and had joined the junior orchestra. For two years, she played the violin for the junior and senior orchestra.

While in junior high school, Swiney-Zoë, discovered her father's story and her grandfather's journal dating back to 1918. Discovering this journal was the start to her interviewing family members and writing her father's story.

For years, she would research the Swiney history.

Swiney-Zoë's father Cesar Swiney taught her how to read the written letter codes he had written in Charles Swiney II's journal. Cesar learned to write in letter codes from his mother Lucy Swiney who was half mulatto (black), and half Seminole.

While attending high school, Swiney-Zoë missed playing the piano. She began playing the piano again and had the opportunity of playing in piano recitals for three years, and winning piano recital awards. Swiney-Zoë won the Minority Scholarship, business award and scholarship.

Swiney-Zoë was an Olympian in Vocational/Industrial Clubs of America (VICA). After attending high school, she attended college and received her degree in Liberal Arts focusing on U.S. and foreign history.

Swiney-Zoë produced a number of unclaimed short stories including, J.F. Scipio: Miles North, J.F. Scipio: Picking Daisies (1985), J.F. Scipio: Jungle Boogie (1992), J.F. Scipio: Three Men from King County (1991), as well as the short story Ulla's Grave (1989). Her past and present research has included, Last of the African Pygmies, and The Nigerian Chief. She received the Dean's

Award in Liberal Arts, focusing on Africana Studies. Swiney-Zoë had been an active political volunteer for Organizing for America.

Swiney-Zoë is one of the original founding members that helped formed the California State University, Dominquez Hills (CSUDH) Veterans Alliance and served as secretary for two years. She serviced as a Volunteer Leader for the Older Adult Center (OAC).

Creator
Maryalice Swiney-Zoë
J.F. SCIPIO SERIES
LOOK FOR THE DRAMA. DISCOVER THE
MYSTERY.

J.F. SCIPIO
PICKING DAISIES

Sometimes it is not best to destroy transparency.

www.ingramcontent.com/pod-product-compliance
Lightning Source LLC
LaVergne TN
LVHW041213080426

835508LV00011B/947